POETRY MATTERS

For Better And For Verse

Essays on the art and craft of
writing poetry by

SARA M. ROBINSON

Poetry Columnist for *Southern Writers
Magazine* and the Suite T Blog

"Set your heart on fire with poetry"

POETRY MATTERS
For Better And For Verse
Copyright © 2022 by Sara M. Robinson. All rights reserved.

Cedar Creek Publishing
Charlottesville, VA

Printed in the United States of America.
Library of Congress Control Number 2022942488
ISBN 978-1-942882-06-0

Photos by the author.

DEDICATION

To my wonderful partner, Carolyn.

To these amazing writing friends for their support:
Linda Layne
Susan Reichert
Al Mermelstein
Carol Cutler
James Cole

And to the many others who have included me in their lives:
You are loved and admired

TABLE OF CONTENTS

Foreword 7
Introduction 8
Why Poetry Matters.. 10

HOW POETRY WORKS FOR US 13

What is Poetry.. 14
What Does Poetry Do?... 16
Why Do I Write Poetry 18
The Blank Page Is to a Poet... 20
When We Create a Poem 22
Driving the Car That Is Our Poetry 24
Using Poetry to Come to the "Great Understanding" 26
Staying Within the Context of Our Writing 28
What's New Is Old; What's Old is New 30
The Thought of Poetry, Or I've Been Sitting Here 32
Cheer Up! Things Could Be Verse..................................... 34
The Reception of Poetry.. 36
When Do We Write What We Know or See?..................... 38
The Poetry of Witness 40
I Sure Like Your Style 42
How Did This Setting Get Me Into This Situation? 44
Clichés – Much Ado About Everything 46

WRITING POETRY IS AN ADVENTURE 49

Why Do (Some) People Hate Poetry................................. 50
Is That Really a Bad Poem, Or Do I Not Get It? 52
Those Are My Words. No. They Are My Words............... 54
Originality in Our Poetry 56
The Education of a Poet 58
Am I Too Old to Start Writing Poetry?............................. 60
How Do We Seize the Moment? 62
How to Keep From Being Distracted… 64
Space, A Writer's Frontier 66

WHAT CATCHES US ON FIRE 69

Poetry as the Mechanism For Seeing Into the Life of Things.... 70
Fire in Your Belly 72
What Is It Really That We Want Poetry to Say? 74
What Sparks Poetry? 76
Can We Put Poetry to Good Use for Others? 78
Birdwatching: Poetry as Telescope Making............................ 80
Energy: The High Bar for Poetry 82
Poetry as a Spiritual Exercise 84
The Purpose of the Evangelical Poet 86
Poetry as Architecture: We Are Builders & Engineers 88
Poetry & Philosophy 90
Why Do We Care About How Poems Come About? 92
Why Do We Envy Other Poets? 94
What is the Worth of My Writing? 96
Humorous Poetry 98
What is Poetry, & Does This Count as It? 100
Normal Size of a Poem 102

LET'S GET MECHANICAL

The Voice of Poetry 106
Lines of Poetry, Part I 109
Lines of Poetry, Part II 111
Form & Work of the Poem 113
The Movement of Poetry 115
The Image in Poetry 117
Wanted Words, Alive-Not Dead, Part I 119
Wanted Words, Alive-Not Dead, Part II 121
Metaphor & Simile 123
Words & Poetry 125
Language & Poetry 127
The Definite in the Indefinite 129
Poetic Diction 131
Concreteness & Abstraction in our Poetic Language 133
Interpretation 135
What I Mean Is... 137
Relationships Within Poetry 139
Honorable Intentions 141
Mimesis-Act of Expression 143

My Poem as a Classic 143
Epic Proportions 147
Lyric Outlasts Everything 149
The Gist of the Subject 151
The Turn 153
Moving Closer to the Close 155
Revision, or I Have a "Write" to Change My Mind 157
Revision, Part II. Write, Re-Write, Right 159
Crossing the Finish Line 161
Finding the "Write" Title(s) For Your Poem(s) 163

AT LAST **165**

The Defense of Poetry 166
Turning the Poem Over to the Poem 169
To Workshop or Not to Workshop: Is that a Question? 171
Engagement with Poetry 173
Am I Done With This Poem 175
How to Conduct a Reading of Your Poetry 177
When We Wrap Works Up and Move On 179

SUGGESTED READING **181**
Some of What's in my Library

MORE ABOUT THE AUTHOR **182**

FOREWORD

Sara M. Robinson will tell you she came to the craft of poetry late in life. But when you read her poetry, you will see as I do, she has always been a poet in her heart.

She creates words of poetry on paper just as an artist creates pictures on canvas

I have had the privilege of knowing Sara for over ten years. Her love of poetry brought her to *Southern Writers Magazine* as a columnist, introducing to our writers, of fiction and non-fiction, the writing of poetry. I was always amazed how her articles of writing opened the world of poetry to young and old, new, and experienced writers alike. And how teaching us about writing poetry made us better writers of our own genres.

Sara told me writing poetry helps you see yourself better, it leads to a depth of yourself not known before. She also teaches that poetry can open a new world, making us better as a people; and through this perhaps we can appreciate and understand the role that literature played in our history. Truly there is a sincerity in poetry.

I am thrilled Sara has written this book, *Poetry Matters*. It truly will give everyone a look into the world of poetry as well as take them on a great adventure. You will have the opportunity to see how poetry works and builds a fire within the writer as well as the person.

Only Sara could have written this enlightening adventure in poetry.

>By **Susan Reichert**, retired Editor-in-Chief of *Southern Writers Magazine*; Co-Publisher of Southern Writers Magazine; owner of Suite T, the Authors Blog. Author of *Listen Close, Between Me and You, God's Prayer Power,* and *Storms in Life.*

INTRODUCTION

Some years ago, when I started writing poetry, Linda Layne (Cedar Creek Publishing), my publisher, suggested I contact Southern Writers Magazine to see if they would be interested in a poetry column. The idea was that I could increase my name recognition more widely and increase my writing skills. What a fantastic suggestion that turned out to be! I met via email, Susan Reichert, Publisher and Editor, along with Gary Fearon, copy editor at the time. They were receptive to the idea and thus I launched my column, *Poetry Matters*. For about nine years we ran about 6-8 columns per year, then when Susan decided to end the magazine and focus on her blog, *Suite T,* I was invited to continue with that. All in all, this has been a most amazing writing experience and an even more amazing friendship. Susan has given me so much exposure for my poetry books and columns I could never repay her for the generosity. She also gave me a venue to promote my love of poetry with hopes for instilling that same love in others. Above all, I can tell you she is my friend for life.

Here is what you can expect to find in this book. I am sharing my philosophy and basic craft ideas with you. I offer tips, suggestions, examples, and encouragement. What I do not do is tell you how to write a poem. There are plenty of books for that. I am trying to reach your poetry heart and liberate any constraints you might have about poetry.

I was not always a poet. I spent thirty-five years in the industrial chemical and minerals mining industries, starting from lab positions and working my way up to vice-president and product management. I published prolifically in these industries, even gaining a patent. But that was then. Though I thrived while working, I didn't realize how much I didn't know, and what I had missed, until I started writing creatively. I took a creative writing course, wrote my first book, a memoir, then accidentally fell into writing poetry. That fall knocked me "conscious." Yes, conscious. I discovered not only poetry, but I discovered myself. I liked the new me much better.

Poetry is the art of discovery and wonder. In my writing years since, I have embraced discovery and wonder, from simple lines to complex works. You will see many references to nature, especially since I live beside the Rivanna River. It is a writing muse for me. Poetry and rivers have a big thing in common: They both are always moving. And I have been discovering and wondering ever since. That is my sincere desire for you with this book.

If you want to check out more of my future essays, then go to the Suite T Blog - southernwritersmagazine.blogspot.com

Give yourself a chance and go on this marvelous adventure: Poetry, It's for better and for verse.

All the best,
Sara

Why Poetry Matters

On a sunny, unremarkable day, I see poetry lying in an ordinary ditch, beside a nondescript road. Everybody walks past it, taking no notice. The poetry can't shout out, nor can it jump, but it's still alive. So, I think as I jump in and attempt to save poetry, I have to be a Good Samaritan. This has to be a calling for me and a purpose. Then, I pondered, we need more Good Samaritans to save poetry. We can't leave poetry to lie about, especially if it is falling into inaccessible places. Poetry matters and it is up to all of us to tell everyone.

I was reminded recently of the fragility of poetry's survival when Alexandra Petri's article appeared in The Washington Post. She made excellent points about whether poetry is dead or alive. She, along with many of us poets, and I hope a lot of listeners, was taken by Richard Blanco's inaugural poem. What appealed to me most about his poem were the same gifts that poetry still offers: strong visuals, exemplary language, tingling senses, and the anticipation of all worldly things. When a great poem, such as his "One Today," is given to the public, we humble receivers are exposed to what poems are all about, and why they matter.

Poems from the ages, such as *The Iliad, the Odyssey*, and Dante's *Inferno,* were required reading for most of us years ago, when (I bet) we just wanted them to be over. Who can recall great lines that inspired men to war, women to love, and societies to exist? Too bad great poetic forms have competed against raging hormones, football games, and now, insistent smart phones. Likely the poetry app is not the most downloaded app for tweens, young adults, or even those my age.

How do we convince the public—our vast community— that poetry matters? Well, for starters, we poets have to get out more. And I mean we have to step out of our usual comfort zones, which for many is the college classroom. We have to find public readings and show up prepared to read. We must read not just our own stuff, but the poetry of others. We need to create a reading space if nothing is available. For instance, contact the owner or manager of your favorite coffee shop and ask him if he would like to hold an "open mic" event. This brings in customers, so I'm sure he'll go for it. Try this at libraries, too. Join local writing groups and workshops. Ask to be on the program. Most of these organizations serve the local writing public and would love to interact with the larger writing community. Go to middle schools, high schools, and community colleges, too. Go back to your home town and offer to do a public reading at the local community center.

If you can see where I am going here, then you can tell my fear is that poetry will lose the audience which popularized it in the beginning—the public. Sure, we need academia, and I'm happy for all of the brainy literary types who continue to publish their poetry. But for whom are they publishing? Let's get our poets out among us plebeians who don't necessarily read the literary (read collegiate-based) journals. One way we can do this is to clamor for more anthologies or community-based journals and magazines. We can seek out and support small independent presses which publish anthologies for local- based writing groups. This makes poetry a community event. We need to get academics more involved in our community, not we more involved in theirs.

We need to write to newspapers and magazines and ask them to publish poetry. When poetry competes with politics, humor, sports, and food, then everyone wins. Poetry might be thriving in the journals and papers for the literary professionals, but no one in the mainstream reads them. We need to show our "community" the riches of Kay Ryan, Naomi Nye, Wallace Stevens, William Carlos Willams, and Sherman Alexie. And not all of these were or are the strict academics.

When poets were part of the entire "artist" world, their lives were part of ours. We smiled during the 1950's and 1960's at the bohemian lifestyles and the "beatnik" personas. But we watched and listened and were engaged because the poets themselves were engaged with us. When did poets get separated from us? How did we demand that poets become academics? By corralling them into colleges and universities, we "institutionalized" poetry, creating an elitist, almost separatist society. We didn't do that to our musicians. I don't see Beyonce teaching a college course on music theory or lyric writing, yet her words are recited by lots of people. On the other side, Sheryl Crow has been known to go to her local schools and teach piano.

There now exist agents who arrange, for a substantial fee, speaking engagements for academic poets. The former poets laureate and other well-published poets can command fees up to and exceeding $15,000 to talk about their poetry. That's a lot of car washes for a community to afford a poetry reading from a big name.

Until we bring poetry back to the streets, in a sense, we are not going to successfully answer why poetry matters. The lyrics, tones, and narratives of poems that can move the public to not only think great thoughts, but also live great moments will be lost. Poetry will fall into those ditches.

I leave you with this: We will always have scientists, mathematicians, and physicists to prove how big the universe is, how far away stars are, how small particles are, and how old the Earth is. We'll have philosophers to tell us why things exist, and explain why we are. But we will always need poets to tell us why all of this matters.

And now let's delve into the matters…

HOW POETRY WORKS FOR US

What Is Poetry?

Inspired by a recent essay asking this same question, I started thinking more about all that I have written about poetry, as well as the poems I have composed. After all, what is this genre we are writing? I guess we could ask the other long questions, too. Why? How? Where, and When might be a little obscure as to poetry, but back to the first question: What is poetry?

Is poetry prose, simply written differently? Some poetry critics say that poetry is simply prose broken up into short lines. Really? That's an over simplification of the most amazing literary genre that the human brain has created. There is method to poetry and the first step is compaction: every word must serve a purpose. Even prose poetry (to further confuse matters) has specific tasks, such as creative visuals. Poetry also relies on a peculiar kind of rhythm to state its case for being poetry. The rhythm or cadence can seem musical or it can match the rhythm of human speech. Poetry does not have to have rhyming lines, but the language must be true.

Writing of true, I emphasize that language must be true in that it represents a keen interest and application of words. This is not the same as truth. My mantra is: Poetry can always be fiction, but the words must reveal great truths. By means of example, Alexis de Tocqueville wrote in his seminal *Democracy in America,* " …men in democracies, whose concerns are in general so paltry, call upon their poets for conceptions so vast and descriptions so unlimited." These authors undertake such grand requests and respond with the gigantic to reach the multitudes. The risk is that poets get so lofty that they simply float away.

Poetry is the relevant genre of our times as well. We see in currently published works the anxieties, horror and redemptions that mankind faces. The world is brought closer to us and our own local geography is put right in front of us. Poetry is a mirror. Its reflections are created by words that make us either think, cringe, laugh or cry. At its best, poetry is a call to action. How? Remember Amanda Gorman and her poem, "The Hill We Climb"?

Poetry is the all-inclusive "WE" for this planet. Poetry is more than a tie that binds, it is the rope of salvation. A rescue ship whose constant search is for more of us to save.

What is poetry? Perhaps the answer is what poetry is not.

Keep writing…

What Does Poetry Do?

Recently I have seen articles asking their readership to answer: What does poetry do? I also asked my poetry critique group this question. One of my poetry friends responded, when asked if poetry can "fix" the world, responded with "poetry is not a screwdriver." Poetry is not supposed to fix anything.

Or is it? If we define "fix," as setting something right that may have been incorrectly placed or to make something permanent or stable, then maybe poetry can fix at least something.

I'm advocating that poetry can be a "universal fixer." What I mean is this: If the creation of poems can persuade an adversary to reconsider a point, create an awareness for an individual who has never appreciated the blueness of a particular bird, or offer an empathetic view toward diversity, to name just a few, then I think poetry can do many things. Poetry itself is not in the doing. Poetry is in the thinking and then we do the doing.

Witness (no poetry pun intended) recent events of violence. We have seen much come out of the writing community on topics of policing, inequalities of service, statues that resurrect unimaginable times, and so on. When I read poetry and articles about certain events, I am not looking for clues to fix something. I am looking for emotional commitment to the topic. If someone is that moved to write about it, then I know that person wants to offer a "fix." The poet Brenda Hillman uses the word "metonymy" to draw an association with realism. For example, "The White House today raised up rails around the east side," or "the Giants need a new glove in right field." Here is one from me: "Detroit needs to remove the tarnish it has inherited." Now while these lines are not poetic, what they give us is a way for poetry to do something. That is to say, we can take a collective, have it provide the action, or possibly a way to be fixed.

Another view of what poetry can do: Poetry can intimate that the past is never quite over with. This line, taken from poet, Matthew Bevis, sums it up: "Did you just get *déjà vu*?" The implication here is that we are reading a poem about something that happened and the reader knows that something similar happened to them, too. I have had times when a stranger has come up to me, drawing attention to some poem I wrote, then telling me that they were either at that same place or had that same feeling. How did I know or do that? While I want to say that poetry is magical, that seems flippant. Of the things that poetry can do, what it cannot do is perform magic.

When you write your poems, think about what poetry is doing for you at that time. Maybe you just saw something that moved you so much you cried. Was it for joy? Sorrow? What if you wrote about your feelings? That is when poetry does something.

Until next time!

Why Do I Write Poetry?

In the past years, I have written columns and essays about the craft of writing poetry. Like a lot of writing, poetry is a very personal thing to do. In fact, the composition of poetry may be the most personal of literary genres, more so than autobiography. I submit this statement because in poetry there is an expectation that we are creating an art form of verbiage. This art form has a unique shape, and must present its arguments (if you will) in a compact way. An autobiography, on the other hand, can let loose for hundreds of pages and reveal everything the author wants. In poetry often there is much left unsaid, so that what is not there can creep, crawl, thrash or thunder its way in. That is the essential seduction of poetry. And it is why many of us write poetry.

Poets are keenly tuned to their surroundings, real or imaginary. It is the awareness and sensitivity that forms the basic core of their writing. I write because I sense wonder about all that goes on around me. I wonder about the past. I wonder about the people I grew up with and what they are doing now. I wonder why people act the way that they do, whether with good intentions or not. I wonder about my future; will I continue to be happy or not. There have been poets who wrote of many troubles in their lives and how so personal everything was around them. We've categorized them as "confessional" poets. Witness Sylvia Plath, Anne Sexton, and a current one I know, Angela Carter. Many poets write about survival of trauma in hopes that readers will empathize and feel connected in some way. Many poets write about the wonder of nature and how its beauty, for example, grants us pleasure and a sense of connectedness to the earth.

I write to impart information and to invite readers to share that information with me. But I write using language that is more attuned to engaging the senses rather than simply reporting an observation. If I want my readers to feel my wonder at something or to connect in a deep way, then I believe I must wordsmith my writing that draws them in.

Here is an opening line from one of my published poems:
"He dreams of wild wests, sorrelled ponies, cowboyed boots and prairied homes where ranged voices sing of fun…"
In this line I even make up new words to create the visual. That's another reason to write poetry. If I can't find the perfect word, since there are no rules, I can create one to serve my purpose!

Ask yourself, "Why do I write poetry?" Then smile, you know why you do.

The Blank Page Is To a Poet As a Blank Canvas Is To a Painter

Both start with a figurative "blob" on the space. In the case of poets we start when we put the pen point to the paper and thus begin. Even if you don't use paper anymore, when you tap that key and it puts down that first letter you have started your work.

For now let's take another approach: what do we want that blank or white space to do for our poem? How can we use space as a means of conveying expression that can equal the written words? We embrace our craft fully when we accept that the clever use of space is as active as the words. We are familiar and already practice the "caesura" by the use of punctuation and sounds. But we can use white space to create a "pause" in the movement, thus giving both the poet, and then the reader, a place to breathe, maybe contemplate.

One favorite poet, James Dickey, read this poem, "The Strength of Fields," at Jimmy Carter's inauguration. Here is how he used white space in this excerpt:

"Of fields.   The solar system floats on
     Above him in town-moths.
                         Tell me, train-sound,
     With all your long-lost grief,   what I can give."//

It is important in a meditative or deep-reaching poem, I believe, to create stress. This is how to bind the reader to the poem. But with the stress, at some point, there must be relief. This can be accomplished in several ways, including brief word couplets (ala William Carlos Williams, also famous for enjambment). When we take control of the speed of the poem, another source of potential stress, we guide the reader toward relief and therefore satisfaction. Try my example:

> Her hair
> fell in   cascades
> of emeralds
> and rubies
> to   land
> on his   hands
> where it   burned

Now with this tidbit of a poem we have some options: we can invoke the senses to offer a mystery. For example at the end, we see the beautiful hair, land; but then this hair did something the reader was not expecting. So, while we had built up some tension/stress, we offered a kind of relief, but then now the reader should want more. Unspoken parts, incremental incidences, are not here, are they? So, we can take the poem further and decide what can we do with the remainder:

> he didn't move   these burns
> seared not   his skin
> but   this one time
> this once   a sear   burned
> his heart.

What has the use of space in this poem done to provide a reality? Was it effective? What would you do differently? Try this poem as an exercise and see where you land…in space.

Keep writing!

When We Create A Poem

What makes a human being make a poem? And I intentionally used the word, "make." To write is one aspect, but to make or create really puts the horse ahead of the cart. What makes a human being treat the creation of a poem as important or at least in the same vein as creating or making a piece of art?

So far in the previous columns, all the mechanics and commentaries about the structure and construction of poetry have added up to really one thing: A creative representation of ourselves expressed as poetry. Doing this is no less complicated or hard than any other craft or talent. Sure, I could argue that piano lessons could lead to an accomplished pianist, but many forego a formal training because they simply want to entertain themselves or a circle of friends. Writing poetry can be accomplished with either formal training or without. However, it does help to read a lot of poetry from a lot of poets, particularly notable ones. And this is if one wants to expose her writing to a larger audience than herself. That's one of the reasons I write this column. While these offerings certainly don't replace some great mentoring, work-shopping with the pros, or even studying in an academic venue, sharing learned experiences contributes to better poetry writing all around. A rising tide floats all ships.

The great Keats once wrote in a letter, " It is easier to think about what Poetry should be than to write it…" That is so true. Like any art, though, practice is the rule. Practice. Envision. Practice. Practice. Edit. Revise. Think "PEPPER." A way to "spice" up your writing.

Look at the poem, "Black Poured Directly into the Wound," by Patricia Smith (see *Poetry* Feb. 2017, page 471). Here we have a moderate length prose poem which some might say is more prose-like than poem-like. "Grief's damnable tint is everywhere." What a powerful line! I say more about prose poetry in a separate column. However, in this case we have a poet telling us, in a 3rd person narrative, a very descriptive tragic story about death of an African-American boy and a mother's reaction to it. This story could be about anyone's mother who sees a child die at the hands of another. Put in the context of witness (see a related column) we are taken right into what we read frequently in the news. Does this work as art? Does this work as poetry? You bet it does both: words "paint a picture," and as poetry it makes us uncomfortable and makes us think. What if this poem had been created as a result of a powerful photograph? Both works of art now.

When we write/create our poetry, we affirm the existence of art. Our art becomes a component of our legacy. How will you create your art?

Driving The Car That Is Our Poetry

In a previous column I talked about why I write poetry. Since then I've given thought as to how I began to write poetry, or how do I begin. Because as a poet I can't resist the metaphor or simile, I compare this thought to learning to drive a car.

Each of us has to get our own individual learner's permit. We issue it to ourselves and we do our own evaluating. Even if we write in academic settings, our teacher is our driving instructor, but we do the driving. Some of us start practicing for the permit when we are quite young, maybe six. Some of us start much later, maybe in our sixties. Then the fun begins. No matter the age, we look at "the driver's manual" that is our guide. An example of a popular manual is Robert Pinsky's, *The Sounds of Poetry*. Another manual is *Beautiful and Pointless* by David Orr. What do we see in manuals? Ah, there are lots of ways to park, make the proper turn, give signals, check the mirrors, etc. We can see lots around us as we move, too: our home, brothers, sisters, sidewalks, books, violins, the boardwalk, the drugstore… More and more we make note of these. Maybe we started a journal or diary. We will make a few stupid mistakes. Parallel parking is tough so we practice, practice, until we get it right. Revise, revise, revise.

We have all this energy and as we practice with our permit we keep our eyes on the "lines." Some will be short; some will be long. Words might be "roadblocks," but they are "bridges," too. We look through our "windshield" with a sense of wonder. Then our imagination takes off. We slow down for a flower or speed up through a heart-break. Still we drive.

A road seemingly to nowhere becomes a fascinating lyric about how we broke a heart one evening while watching for the green flash. Lying in a hammock on someone's farm can be a lament about a wasted life. What if you wrote about a time in your life, in your hometown, with the vision seen only through your rearview mirror? How would you do this? To write about some part of your life as reflected backwards, and how with a simple turn you could then face the windshield.

We don't leave this car. With our foot on the gas, we know we have to move what on some days is a stubborn clunker, but on others is this magnificent, sleek, compact, efficient "charger." Do you have any trips planned?

Using Poetry To Come To the "Great Understanding"

Is poetry a creator of fiction? Is fiction only supposed to be in writing genres such as science fiction, the great American or Southern novel, or romance? Can poetry offer fantasy, horror, thrillers, and crime? I say yes it can. We can take forms of poetry, such as prose free verse, sonnets, and formal (as in terza rima cantos) and create marvelous fiction. And I am not saying anything new here. Witness: Homer, Dante, and Poe.

But I want to talk about today: the contemporary or modern poet who wants to create a fictitious storyline and have it considered poetry at the same time, enough so that within this story, what emerges is the grand goal of poetry (in my opinion): a truth is revealed. I can see an imaginative poet composing a long narrative poem, of great epic proportions, in which she or he actually discusses the horror of some real-life event. The fictional tale is the vehicle and the metaphor is the fuel. The driver is the poet who uses creative language laid out as taut lines, incredible words, and "revelationary"(my word!) premises. How special this would be and how appropriate to achieving a "great understanding" of incredible valid work that poetry can do.

In the imagination of the poet, she or he can conjure up remarkable words that often don't find a suitable place in writing, place them in strategic locations, compel them to do hard work, and then sit back to wait for a reader's response. We lost recently a wonderful poet, C.D. Wright. She was the mistress of the complex one- and two-syllable words, such as nonplussed (one of my favorites because it is so often misused), shunning, and gloms. But this is only one part of her genius. She brought us to the civil rights movement with her poetry book, *One With Others,* that while it is fiction, gives us an understanding of what poetry can do when it speaks a great truth. Another great crafted piece is Lesley Wheeler's *The Receptionist and Other Tales.* Using her technical prowess and incredible story-telling talent, she gives us fiction to reveal great truths, such as defining justice.

We can use our poetry to either put down roots or to swim the message to other shores. Either way we propagate the message. Either way we can influence the local geography and populace. As poets we can listen to the stories unfolding around us, take notes in our journals, think on the majesty of what we heard, and then begin the formation of something big. We start word-by-word, then line-by-line, stanza-by-stanza, then page-by-page. Before our eyes, our fiction becomes a truth, a way to a "great understanding." Our readers will love us for it.

Staying Within the Context of Our Writing

In a previous column, I talked about how poetry can bring readers to great understandings. I used book-length poetry as an illustration of this point. But I want to emphasize that it is quite prevalent that book-length poems are composed of shorter poems that act as "chapters." Think *Olive Kitteridge,* which uses short story-like chapters to build the thread that is the novel. This is how one fiction author maintained the context. A poetry book can do the same thing.

What do we mean, then, when we hear that a poet has strayed from the meaning or context of his or her poetry? Did the writer somehow fall asleep at the wheel, or take a wrong turn, or continue on a path that seemed to go nowhere? Sometimes we get so much in our heads that we forget we are writing a poem. Our poems have become "miniature essays." Now we have gone so far that we have left no work for the readers. We have taken from them the fun of the chase for meaning and insight within the poem.

Poetry composition is the art of compression and contraction. One exception: Prose poetry, which I'll talk about later. Back to writing succinctly. If we want to draw our readers into our heads, thereby opening theirs, then crisp words, sharp visuals, compact lines, and accessible concepts create reader validity. The reader will delve into the context. Another way to keep the context up front is to use space to enhance the poem's presentation on the page. Just like a painter who uses space to focus on the central piece on the canvas, we can use space as a substitute for speech or to take a breath. This is another key to writing good poetry. One of the best presentations of context, and space, is of Adrienne Rich's poem, "Diving into the Wreck," one of the most anthologized of contemporary poems. Her line lengths, language, and space placements between stanzas draw us right in with the diver as she descends to view the old shipwreck. One can "see" the colors of the ocean change, as she goes deeper. Notice these incredible lines from one stanza:

"And now: it is easy to forget
  what I came for
  among so many who have always
  lived here
  swaying their crenellated fans
  between the reefs
  and besides
  you breathe differently down here."

She tells us why she is there and then shows us "the fouled compass," as the poem continues to unfold. Putting an adventure into the context of a truth, revealing how an intrusion, when we are out of our own comfort zone, gives the reader a way to explore his own thoughts. Context. How wonderful when we stay within it.

What's New Is Old; What's Old Is New

Is all the good poetry writing/composition used up? Are we simply revising what is already out there? How can we tell if we are writing anything new?

Recently I was in a Sanibel, FL bookstore that specializes in mysteries. Their selection is enormous and global in scope. I wondered, though, if there is still an original mystery out there to be solved. How many ways to commit a murder, and solve it, are there, after all? The poetry section, by contrast, was rather small with shelves occupied by the usual suspects (i.e. Frost; Collins; Charles Wright; Dickinson, etc.). Actually their selection was the best I had seen in some time.

But like mysteries, I wondered if Frank Bidart wrote all that different poetry from John Ashbery or Elizabeth Bishop. My academic friends could argue for a great course on Originality in Poetry with Comparisons and Contrasts. However, I want to focus on us. We write about feelings, events, observations, etc., that are in our immediate spheres of influence. Our own originality. The key for us, then, must be language. We must strive for uniqueness with our words that fit and then work for us in lines, stanzas, etc. Putting this with our syntax should result in identification as an original poet. And to pile on this, our role as an original Southern poet is emphasized. I'll bet that there is a Southern poet out there who could create a masterpiece, inspired by Wallace Stevens, and has the title: "Nineteen Ways of Looking at a Catfish." The first part (I): "Down along Mossy Creek / Something shimmers in late sun /A twelve-pound catfish lies dying." Now if we take this part and expand it through eighteen more parts, we could develop a Southern tale of perhaps deceit or remorse or something hidden a long time ago, now revealed. What if someone finds that catfish, takes it home, cuts it open, and finds a locket in it? And what if that locket had a picture of the writer's grandmother in it, and this same locket was worn by a favorite daughter who had disappeared? Could this be an original poem written as a Southern gothic mystery? What if the poem ended without the mystery being solved? Would it still be satisfying? Just some thoughts here. I'm using this as an example of plenty of originality out there, but we have to be more and more creative so our works can stand alone. Take this and run with it:

"Absent the fifth string
he still played his greasy-skinned banjo
as if it were a Stradivarius violin.
It was that priceless—
but kind of like whistling
between missing teeth,
something was a little off."

See if you can conjure up something new from something old, perhaps your own mystery.

The Thought of Poetry, or I've Been Sitting Here Thinking About What I Want to Write

Like other genres, it is rare that the poetry writer sits down and immediately composes some extraordinary or even ordinary poetic piece. Many of us keep journals so that phrases, words, snippets of this or that, can have a temporary home until we find a way to use them. I call mine the beginnings of my thought process. From the ephemera on my journal pages, I hope to make something significant and lasting.

Of the many common topics for poetry, one common one is death, or even more specific, grief. Can grief be so huge that it obliterates the loss to nothingness? If death is a black hole, does the star crossing over into it lose everything it was? We likely cannot write about grief, before it was grief; we only can write about it once grief is upon us. To take grief, and make it a poem topic, can be a large challenge to us as we put together something to express it.

How will you, in putting your thoughts into the subject of grief, make your thoughts sufficient enough that you unfold an origami-constructed coffin, peer inside, and react to this corpse that holds your emotions? Will your thoughts come out of a confession (strong, emotional involvement) or an observation (passive observer)?

A topical poem on grief has to convey the poet's role in the work. Writing about grief can't be a spectator sport. You are either in it completely, thus the poet, or not. Because if you are not, then it's a journalistic piece, and you are no more than a reporter. You may not want to go the confessional route (ala Plath or Sexton), but you can model your works around C.D. Wright or William Carlos Williams. He gave us a telling opening line: "sorrow is in my own yard…" In my first poetry book, I wrote about the grief I felt in visiting my parents' graves in my old hometown. It was a very emotional moment for me when I began to write about it. My opening stanza of the poem, "Leaving Elkton," began: "I cried, then sighed, at their graves. / Deep in the earth, in their private little chambers, / I wondered if they heard me."

We use our words to convey our commitment to the topic of a particular poem. Having fully invested and committed, we can show our readers how we really want them to touch our grief, and delve into the poem with us. What word or words can you find deep within your own thoughts to draw people in with you?

Cheer Up! Things Could Be Verse...

Here are two questions for you: Do you have to be sad or depressed or angry to write good poetry? Does how you feel determine your subject matter?

I often read articles by other poets and essayists in which they discuss how mood or state of mind influences their writing. Poets, as a historical bunch of writers, often brag they are in touch with all that surrounds them; and this plays a huge part in their subjects. I think this is very true, but often we are not in a physical or even mental place where we can create poetic lines. This is where my writing journal comes in. I jot down how I feel or how the particular setting affected me, then later I come back to it to write.

Now, however, when I come back to the writing, my mood is no longer the same. For me, the return to my notes is more objective, less subjective or emotional. I don't mean to say less involved; I only present to you that now the poetic part of my brain is "translating" the emotional part I felt at the time into worthy lines.

Meditative poems are examples, I think, of where you might experience a real emotional connection to the writing. Say, you lost a beloved pet, and you wanted to write about your feelings, but you simply were too saddened to compose. You let your mind and soul grieve, then you make some notes which later become the beautiful lines.

I've seen a lot of angry poems. One I read recently was from a poet who was particularly upset about a poetry class he was in. He was very angry at the instructor. This poet thought the instructor did not pay enough attention to him.

So, this poem, to me, was more of a poison pen letter than a creative rendering. Maybe the poet should have used that version as notes and then created a poem about the heartbreak of disappointment or rejection. When you release your writing to the public, then you have engaged them, good or bad.

It can be tricky determining your emotional state and then turning it into poetry. What do you want your writing to do? Wallace Stevens wrote a poem, "Poetry is a Destructive Force."
His first stanza goes like this: *"That's what misery is, / Nothing to have at heart. / It is to have or nothing./..."* He goes on to use animals as metaphors to portray the violence man can have. But the poem is quiet, contemplative. That's what makes his poem so good.

Think about your feelings and how you want to put them into verse. " I felt the coldness of time when my mother died. / Then I saw the sky, and felt warm suddenly…"
S. Robinson

Until next time…

The Reception of Poetry

How does a poem convey its message? It seems the answer would be simple. But it is not. The key is "how." In previous columns we have focused on language and it is definitely a key component. But what about the tone of the language? We have to take in the details of description, action, language, and form. And then we have to construct them in such a way that we have presented a theme, presented the support of it, and then come to a satisfactory end. It is necessary during this process that we do not allow our poem to undermine itself. In other words, we don't want a reader to possibly conclude that this poem was written badly because he or she failed to interpret it like the poet intended.

What about the pace of the poem? If we are using details of observation or emotional reaction, we should slow down enough so these are observed and contemplated by the reader. Some techniques include line breaks, enjambment, white space, and punctuation. One notable writer has suggested that the space surrounding the poem, that space where we breathe and speak is as important as the space occupied by the poem itself. What does this mean? How do you interpret that suggestion? Well, let's think about this. To me the maven of space and line placement is Rae Armantrout. In her award-winning poetry book, *Versed*, she has such incredible lines and the use of white space is nothing short of remarkable. And still I understate. She numbers her stanzas, and each one may only contain a line. In her poem, "Whatever," from this book, try to picture the lines even though I'm having to use hash marks here: "Up and down / the branch / she's twelve, / she's waking up / to herself, / opening / her pairs of / stubby, yellow/ wings."

The poet brings the reader into the poem, perhaps maybe intimidates the reader, but should always make the event (yes, reading poetry should be a very personal event), entertaining and enlightening. Back to "interpretation." One of the fun things you do as a poet is to render your poems "subject to interpretation." That reinforces the experience you expect your readers to have.

So, if among vital components of your poetry, is space and you place this space strategically and beautifully, you and your readers will have fulfilling "aha" moments.

Breathe / then stretch / reach / then sigh / write / then pause / repeat. You did it, didn't you? Think of all you can do with space and time, configured within your poems.

When Do We Write What We Know Or See?

The other day I was asked if I was creating verse about current events, especially since I live in Charlottesville. I replied that I really wasn't. And I thought later, why not? It seems that historically poets who witnessed horrific events were generally compelled to create passionate verse responses. I find that is difficult for me. It is not that I am not moved by catastrophe or living history or social issues. It is mostly about my comfort level. For most of us pastoral poetry is really what makes us live in the moment. By this I mean writing passionate lines about nature with its living creatures.

I'm currently working, for example, on a poem about an injured Canada goose I found this morning on my usual walk. It tried so hard to fly, flapping spastic wings, and falling over backward. It was clear that it was injured in some way. I was moved by its instinct to keep trying. I wondered how that would work as a metaphor for keeping up courage in the face of disaster. That led me to think about the fires of California and the ash remains of homes in which folks lived, read, ate their dinners, and thrived. These fire-broken devastated homes remained as skeletons of a past. Like the goose, their existences were forever changed. I knew that houses could be rebuilt, but I knew that goose would never fly again, and likely would not make it through the night.

How is it that when we write about what we see and feel it is so subjective? Critics of the confessional poets used to admonish them for revealing so much about their personal illnesses and weaknesses. These poets created some of the most impressive and important poetry of the modern centuries. Their illnesses became metaphors for life among others and it was, I believe, their way of bringing illness to the forefront, rather than hidden in the shadows. One big gift a poet can bring is the unwrapping of the present that is within yourself to reveal the core of humanity within everyone.

So, in current events, we see everyday states of affairs that are ever changing and will always do so. Sometimes the changes are rapid; sometimes they are slow. But all of these are part of the human experience. For many poets writing about components of the experience is a personal goal. When poets share some of this with the rest of us, we again have been given a gift. To see things like a mortally-wounded goose, and feel empathy as well as sadness, inspires me to write something about living along side the pain of nature; promising the world that I might be magical somehow, with words, to make that pain a little less.

I guess, then, I do write something about current events after all. Like I wrote in one of my earlier published poems, "sometimes the large is often seen in the small."

Keep writing!

The Poetry of Witness

One of our most admired poets, Carolyn Forché, invented the term "poetry of witness." As a former active writer and observer of human rights, much of her poetry was about seeing inequities of life around her. This brings me to the topic of how we use poetic language to define the present, especially writing about current events. There is this instant, this moment that is between "not yet," and "just happened." This moment is so narrow that we must consider it a metaphorical tightrope or balance beam in which we take careful steps. When writing about something as it is happening, we may use our journals and we may even take on the persona of "reporter." We don't want to rely on secondhand memory for the full effect of what we want to say later when we compose our poetry.

Our observation with its notes will congeal as words and lines which give our readers a place in a certain past that, in the present, they may never visit; but is a place they have lived in all their lives. As poets we will be not only the narrator, but we will provide the temperament of the poetry because it is coming from us with our moods reflected from our observations. And more as poets we create a history from what has been preserved and survives. A great example is poet Nikki Giovanni's Convocation address given on April 17, 2007 at Virginia Tech. This address was actually a poem of witness about the horrible tragedy of the killings of thirty-one students. This poem will forever remain as a powerful reminder of what is now history. Take a look at these lines from the address:

"We are strong enough to stand tearlessly, we are brave enough to bend to cry, and we are sad enough to know we must laugh again."

Each poet has her own present-at that-time-written in a mood which is reflected at that time. To write in the present of an event or even an emotion gives this special character and permanence. I like to think of a poem of witness as being a very short "social novel." In this I mean, a poem set in the present and meant to portray, with a hint of advocacy, a real-life crisis (i.e. political, racial, war). The brevity of the poem contrasted to the length of a novel gives a sense of urgency and immediacy whereby the writer becomes now the emissary for a particular injustice.

So, what will you observe? What will stir your emotions such that you want to pen a great poem? What will you witness that can become a part of history?

I Sure Like Your Style

What does it mean when someone reads your poetry and comments, "I like your style. I understand your poem(s)." That simple comment, given as a compliment, is really an acknowledgment of your investment as a writer. The one offering the compliment may not even know the value of that statement.

Let's give this some attention. If you have committed your writing efforts to creating poetry, there is likely evolving some components of your writing that are unique to your craft. All the practice, all the revisions, all the thoughts, all the research, and all the sweat and frustrations compose the fundamentals of your style. This is your individual mark, like a notary's stamp, that registers your "ownership." You created the piece in your unique way and the "stamp" is your style.

With the creation of your style, you essentially have established your own "greatness." Now all you have to do is convince the reader that he/she is in the presence of this greatness. How to do that? By using language that impresses the reader so much that they are compelled to keep reading. And keep reading your poetry. By writing verse that is so "poetical" as to move the reader to think deeply and enjoyably, you have established yourself as writer of purpose. I have coined what I think is a new term. "Hysterical poeticism." I define this as poetic language that becomes so gossipy it loses its purpose. You don't want to write something and call it poetry simply because you want it to be poetry. You want to embrace narratives that contribute to the great understanding (see an earlier column) and bring imaginative wealth. Your readers become "rich in spirit" as a result of your writing.

William Wordsworth, who we all read in high school, believed that writing poetry should be "man speaking to man." Sure, we may not want to write in the language of Wordsworth today, but you have to admit that "A Humming Bee—a little tinkling rill— / A pair of falcons wheeling on the wing, / In clamorous agitation, /"... is simply beautiful..

A contemporary poet, Maxine Kumin, was inspired by Wordsworth. In her poem, "Poem for My Son," she started the first stanza: "Where water laps my hips / it licks your chin. You stand / on tiptoe looking up / and swivel on my hands./"... Her style of language is so visual, so human, that we believe that with that first line we are standing in the water with her, and cannot wait to see what the little boy does next.

As you construct your style, keep in mind the humanness of your writing. Let this fill with the "colors" that are your signature. What is the first color for you that comes to mind?

How Did This Setting Get Me Into This Situation?

As we have learned, virtually anything can be a subject for a poem. The poet Pablo Neruda said that there were only eleven subjects. Now that is interesting especially since we also know he didn't really provide the list of eleven (that I can find anyway). However, in her book, *The Discovery of Poetry,* Frances Mayes gives us her list of potentials, including "beginnings, memory, art, time," etc. I submit these as they relate the most to the settings/situation topic discussed here.

There are numerous options for settings. What if we are next to a quiet stream. Nothing much happens, but then all of a sudden, we see a water strider tiptoe across the water. Suddenly a large-mouth bass grabs it. All at once we have a situation and we can write about it. We could describe a natural setting, no conflicts, just words about how we feel one with nature. Or we can take this setting and let the situation become a metaphor for something larger in life, *predator vs prey*; now we are witnesses.

As poetry has evolved, types of poems have appeared to especially describe particular settings. Types include pastoral (usually a rural landscape, maybe some sheep); aubade (usually about dawn, maybe a lover who leaves); carpe diem (where the setting is time); and ars poetica (where the poet writes about writing poetry, some situation). There are more but you get the idea.

I think a poem could have master settings and this takes me back to Neruda's eleven subjects. I tend to think there are three "master subjects" for poets: Love, Death, and Themselves. Poets historically take these three, put them into a variety of situations and settings; then reveal and possibly resolve.

In Cesare Pavese's poem, "Grappa in September," this line starts a stanza:

"This early, you see only women. /..." Then he ends with these two lines: "steeping them to their depths in the soft air. The streets / are like the women. They ripen by standing still." Masterful. (from Frances Mayes's book, *The Discovery of Poetry*).

Clichés – Much Ado About Everything

Ah, the challenge of creating new original lines and words, when it's tempting to use lines we have heard and read before. But, I give you a gentle warning: Use clichés in your writing at your peril. If you want your poetry to be accepted; read over and over again; treasured; and, ultimately published, then take the necessary time to be as original as possible. You might ask: Have all the original lines and words been used up? Is everything we read a cliché? Thankfully, no, although sometimes when I am struggling with my writing, I ask that same question.

This brings me to figurative language. As poets, we devote a great deal of energy, time, and no small amount of frustration (I'm sure) to express how we see the fluids of life circulate around us. Let's review what figurative language is. Theodore Cheney (in *Writer's Digest*) gave a great example: "He was a bull in a china shop." This is also an example of metaphor, which we talk about in another column. So, I won't repeat that here. Let's get back to how figurative language keeps us from clichés. And you will notice and agree that Cheney's example above has now become cliché.

Think of the how trademarks became generic products after being used so much in the common language. Kleenex is an example. How to write about life, and nature, and emotions in an original way is tricky for new writers and sometimes even for seasoned writers. A common mistake is to use "mixed metaphors" in our writing. Example: again from Cheney, "Whenever the chips are down, I'll back you to the hilt."

One creative way/technique is to "personify" something that is not human. This can be a very clever and engaging way to write amazing pieces. Recently in a book, *Annals of the Former World* by John McPhee, he was amazed at the old descriptions of geology that to him were simply poetic. I love "starved coastlines," and "drowned rivers." You can bet I will figure out some way to use these. Today in my office, "my desk bears the weight grandly of my thoughts and my laptop, which protests quietly by misspelling my words."

See how you can think of ways to go with your writing. It is raining and with its companion the angry wind, leaves are fighting all around as if each one wants to be first to hit the ground. Our imaginations can go to any extreme we want. All we have to do is let it go. Stuck for words? Read a favorite poet or grab up your dictionary.

Where will your fingers go today with their playmate, the pencil or pen?

NOTES:

WRITING POETRY IS AN ADVENTURE

Why Do (Some) People Hate Poetry?

There must be some type of historical animus toward poetry for at least one notable poet to write a book titled *The Hatred of Poetry*. Its author, Ben Lerner, states that the dislike goes back to our high school days when we were forced to memorize and recite rhyming, formal poetry. I discuss this "hatred" in one way in another essay about writing poetry.

If we are going to write poetry, we certainly want others to read it. So, what do we say when we encounter those who say they hate it? It may not be that they hate it, per se, but that they don't "get it," therefore they don't like it. Some will even go further and say they believe poetry is dead, if not passé.

Ah, the thrown gauntlet; now is our chance. We must hold sway over those skeptics who would deny the reality that poetry is not dead. Today it is more alive than ever. I see more poetry about current events, such as #MeToo, school massacres, politics, war, and ethnic plights, than I have in years. I see young writers pouring out their hearts borne on the backs of compelling language filled with conviction, anger, and hope.

This is where we need to go: We need to take our poetry to lofty stations, not exclusive heights where only a few can climb; but to the bus stations, the town corners, the libraries, schools, and main streets everywhere. We can show people the power of OUR poetry by being visible and accessible. When someone asks us what do we do, we face them squarely and state, "we write poetry." If at first their eyes don't glaze over, then we know we have them. The conversation becomes easier. If they don't "get it," then you can do what I do, invite them to an upcoming reading. Just so you know, I hold many of my readings at distilleries or wineries. These are excellent venues for poetry.

So think about ways you can show and tell about poetry in your community. Let's make sure that there is no hatred or death for this marvelous genre in which we write.

Is That Really a Bad Poem, Or Do I Just Not Get It?

A friend asked me recently, what is the definition of bad poetry? Wow, I thought, this is a tough question. For starters, poetry is so subjective, so personal, that every person has a unique view of what a poem is, good or bad. But maybe there is a way to separate "good" from "bad" poetry.

One resource I found stated a consensus believed that prose is words in their best order, while poetry is the best words in their best order. Many writers believe that poetry demands precision. In other columns I have mentioned conciseness and compactness as important components.

Another thought is that a poem could be "bad" if it lacks a discernible point, and sounds like prose. That last is tricky as prose poetry is a form; and, in reality, few poets can pull this off with success. See the great poetry of Mary Jo Bang and Robert Haas for how successful they are.

What are some key things to look for (as a reader) or avoid (as a writer) in "bad" poetry?
Bad rhymes/forced
Cliché overloads
Too much punctuation (especially exclamation points)
Weak/Ineffective lines
Lacks an interest
No visible point of the poem
Lack of originality
Lack of interesting language/overworked words/misspelled/misused words

Memorably bad poetry is often created by a poet who is unaware of his/her defects. I have read some pretty dreadful poetry. I must admit I have written some pretty dreadful poetry, too. If my work is too awful to be revised or salvaged, into the trash bag it goes. The last thing a writer wants to hear about his/her work is that lofty ambition overcame practical sense, self-confidence was too grand, and incompetence was present in the writing.

A word that critics attach to their description of bad poetry is narcissistic. I interpret this to mean that poets fall into a trap of using mediocre, tired words to describe minor occurrences in everyday life. The poet, Billy Collins, is the only one I know who can take a grocery list and turn it into riveting poetry. The rest of us need to engage with the world at large, avoid 1st person POV, and delight our readers with insightful ideas.

Those Are My Words. No, They Are My Words. The Uncomfortable Topic of Plagiarism

Of the many columns I have written, this could be one of the most difficult. How do we avoid stating the same things others have written? We can't always, but the rub is when we don't give credit where credit is due. Unlike historical non-fiction or fiction, poets likely get away with a lot of copying without attribution. For instance, have you ever seen a list of citations at the end of a poetry book? I mean real citations and credits, not acknowledgements. I bet no one really checks up on poems to see if they are plagiarized in part or in whole, unless it is in academia or a literary critic who is an expert on all poetry. But that doesn't give poets an excuse to steal unabashedly. Every action has a consequence.

So, how do we avoid plagiarism? We often write with books of poetry by our sides. I sure do. I'm looking for inspiration, but I also want the words to be my own. Maybe I am having trouble pulling together powerful words to describe a nest of robins. I might look to Mary Oliver or Robert Frost. Maybe I like their words, but maybe their arrangements don't authenticate me. I let my imagination wander around their lines then I start with a new word. For example, I love Wallace Stevens' "Thirteen Ways of Looking at a Blackbird." But as a Southern writer who likes to write in whimsy sometimes, I looked at his formatting, and came up with my own approach, which I called, "Nineteen Ways of Looking at a Catfish." Is that plagiarism? Well no. But if I had taken direct words or lines of his, put them into my poem, and didn't give him credit, then yes it is.

"To be or not to be" (Shakespeare) original, that is our

choice, but why would we not want to be original? A lot of great verse has been written, but there is still a lot of great original verse yet to be composed. We have overused the term "voice" to describe our own way of expressing ourselves. But the truth is our writing. It has to be our writing.

Don't you want your readers to appreciate your own words?

Originality in Our Poetry

We should discuss language and how to keep it "fresh." We've talked about clichés before, but we should think about how we can keep our writing sharp. If our poetry is to stir emotions and imaginations, then we need to insert words that are not overused, tired, or just plain worked to death. Sometimes I feel that way about punctuation, too. I've read a lot of poetry in which the exclamation point has been used so many times, I think that there are none left in the universe. But we have plenty of seldom-used words that can give us all the power and uniqueness our writing deserves.

To take our notes, cast them like an unfurling umbrella about to face-off a heady wind, is to give them life and visuals to stimulate a reader's appetite. One of my favorite resources is *The Transitive Vampire, A Handbook of GRAMMAR for the Innocent, the Eager, and the Doomed*, by Karen E. Gordon. She challenges me to think of grammar using fantastical, whimsical, and extraordinary nouns, verbs, adverbs, etc. instead of the usual examples. How about these nouns? midwife, alchemist, ruffian, Desdemona, nomad, dilettante, hit-man. In an explanation of verb tense, she offers: Present tense, " I mope alone. Meteors rove the heavens." For past tense, " She moped in the bistro. I moped in my boudoir."

The use of concrete, abstract, and collective nouns offers opportunity to be creative and specific in our poetry. When was the last time you used "plethora" in a poem? I'm not sure I ever have. There are other examples: flask, bog, harpsichord, machete, murder (of crows). I love to study abstract nouns. For example, I still look for a way to use "miasma." Poet Jana Prikryl uses unique word combinations to satisfy her metaphors. To write about clouds and see them as "floating albino basketballs of hydrangea," simply thrills me.

Since we know that metaphor is an essential component of our poetry, this opens up a world of creative language for us. We can take all the liberty we want to be fresh, persuasive, evocative, and succinct. Perhaps incorporating regional syntax along with regional words can give a specificity to location of a poem. I don't encounter the word, "honeybunch," in literature very much, though I hear it all the time at my local diner.

I would probably be more authentic, too, if when writing a poem about the winters of Wisconsin, I inserted, "You betcha," somewhere in the composition.

So, we have options to be original. How will you be original?

The Education of a Poet

Taking some notes and thoughts from the accomplished writer, Edward Hirsch, I now ask the question: Are we born to write? I also would ask, Are we born to write poetry? How do we know poetry is what we want?

I bet that when most of us were growing up we didn't give much thought to a future writing career. I know I certainly didn't. I was too busy riding my bicycle, hanging out with friends, reading comic books, and mostly being a kid. Some of my friends kept diaries and sometimes they would share little rhyming poems they penned. Most of these were little ditties about pretend boyfriends and pets.

At some point, we became writers. Many found it early in life, and many, like me, found writing much later. That's not so unique. Frank McCord didn't publish his inaugural novel *Angela's Ashes* until he was sixty-six. Does that mean we have to wait until we are well passed middle-age before we can write? For some of us, the right side of the brain did not kick in until later in life. For others, it may mean that we were so busy either doing other types of art or we were simply busy with life. Like John Lennon once said something like: " Life happens while you are making other plans." I had an artist friend, who in her late 80s published her first book of poetry. It was a *tour de force*. Extraordinary effort.

This brings me up to a characteristic that is essential to the education. *Ambition.* A strong desire to achieve something. We have to want to write poetry as much as anything else. Why is this so important? Because it is the "driver" of this car we call poetry (See a previous column). We look for the

impetus that gets us up and then gets it done. Ambition will keep us wanting not to fail. And remember, failure is in your perception. No one is judging you or your poetry output. Your writing is not under any intense scrutiny. Your ambition is yours and yours alone. You give yourself permission to define your desire and how much education you want to put into your writing. I love to read poetry, poetry criticism, and pretty much anything that involves poetry.
My personal education is ongoing but that's how I am. You may have a totally different approach and that is great.

Poetry is so individual and so is the education of a poet. A last thought: Keep writing!

Until next time…

Am I Too Old to Start Writing Poetry?

Who says we are too old to write poetry? Not me, for sure. My first published book of poetry came out when I was sixty-two. By that time, I had won a couple of minor, but paying, poetry awards. And, my name got out there to run with the other thousands of poets in the great pack of writers on Earth. It is never too late to start anything you have a mind to do. At least you can try.

What would you need to do to start writing at an advanced (i.e. 55 plus) age? I would recommend you get an AARP card so you can take advantage of hotel, restaurant, and other discounts. Don't laugh. If you go to gatherings of like-minded writers you may need to stay overnight and that discount saves you money. A rational thought as you begin your quest is to not consider this path for a source of income. You may have to decide to self-publish, especially if you are in a hurry to get a book out. You may want to enter your poems in writing contests and most of them charge reading fees. At $10-$20 a submission, this can add up. But the experience of seeing your poems in print or in digital is worth it.

Think about the notable fiction writer, Frank McCourt. He published his first novel, *Angela's Ashes,* when he was sixty-six. While no longer living, he achieved great critical acclaim. While poets like W.S. Merwin, Richard Wilbur, and Donald Hall, began writing poetry in their 20s, they were still publishing poetry and essays well into their 90s.

Here is more inspiration. *Southern Writers Magazine* interviewed the poet, radio host, and renowned playwright, Grace Cavalieri. Her first book of poetry came out when she was forty-three. In 2019 she received one (out of 15) of the inaugural fellowships from the Academy of American Poets. Grace is eighty-seven years old! And you should read her list of accomplishments.

We are not too old to start writing poetry. Make your poetry a grand achievement of your maturity.

How Do We Seize the Moment?

How do we know if a particular moment is the moment to write? Seems like a funny or peculiar question, doesn't it? But take a moment to think about when is the right time or "moment" to compose a poem. I often wonder if I spend too much time waiting for the right moment. Likely I do. Then I find I have frittered away a perfectly good afternoon without anything "poetic" to show for it. Sometimes finding the right moment has to be forced, and that means focusing on the task at hand. Yes, sometimes composing lines can be a task, and that is not all bad. It really depends on how one defines "task."

If you don't think you are in the moment, then ask why not? Sure, the right moment might not be while your hands are in the middle of running the vacuum. But there is that off button, if the moment arises. If you put that off when a great line comes into mental sight, and you decide that it can wait, you'll recall it. Guess what. It doesn't happen.

When you find yourself in your writing space, and nothing is coming forth, take one of your poetry books off the shelf and randomly open to a poem. Say it is Mary Oliver (who doesn't have one of her poetry books?). I just did it, and opened to her poem, "Mushrooms." Read the poem, then zoomed in on a line. I found one: "innocent as sugar…" Now what about something sweet, or maybe the antithesis of sweet. What about sour news from a relative about the loss of their pet, who was so sweet, that…

See how a poem starts to form? This is how you take a moment from all the moments and claim it for yourself. And, give yourself permission for the poem to be short. Not every rendering has to be epic. The most important message here is that you took a momentous opportunity and made something from it, at least a start of something.

"I will miss her
  sweetness and softness
  I will not see
  or feel again."

Until next time…

How to Keep From Being Distracted, or Whoops, I See a Chicken...

Now that you have your writing space, your toolbox of supplies is full, and your energy is right where it needs to be, how do you keep your focus? You have this great plan consisting of poetry themes you want to congeal into some remarkable verse. But you can't settle down. You're at your laptop, hands ready to type, yet you keep gazing around your space. Don't even think about getting up to dust. Instead think about dust particles floating in the light coming in through the window. What a cool metaphor for " little molecules of me drifting in late sunlight."

Your energy needs direction just as much as your poetry does. Stoke that creative fire but keep it within the fire pit. First of all if you are feeling distracted, one way to control it is to start typing or writing randomly. Let your energy through your pen ramble all around the page. Look for anything suspicious that you can use. Keep your eyes on the laptop or paper. Make yourself work hard on this. Turn off your social media sites and put your phone on airplane mode. If you have to let your fingers rest and your mind relax, then time yourself by counting to ten. Start again. Keep starting over. The instant you realize that the workers on the house next door are taking a break, you've seen a chicken.

If you have to, get up and walk around your space. Pick out a book, anything, then come back to your writing, randomly choose a page, type or write the first word you see.

Take that word and write some things you know about it. Ignore articles and prepositions, look for nouns and verbs. I just looked away from my laptop and the first word I saw on my desk was "guilty." I can write tons about that, but let's assume I simply want to know if that dog who pooped on my pansies felt guilty. I saw their pink and yellow colors fade and disappear under a steaming brown mound of organic dung. I felt sad, maybe a little guilty, too. I should have protected them better. I think I'll make up a poem about this.

How about you?

Space, A Writer's Frontier

Do you have a dedicated area for your writing? Where is it? How connected to your regular living environment is your space? It is important for all of us who write to have a "room of our own." We can define that room anyway we want as long as it belongs to us, the writers. No one else should claim it. Even if your space consists of an unfinished door propped up on two sawhorses, it has to belong to you. When you "enter" your space you leave the outside world and let your body and mind go wandering into your imagination.

What comprises your space? Pencils, pens, laptop? Here are my essentials:
Sticky pads, various sizes
3 x 5 index cards
Pencils, pens, highlighters, erasers, laptop, printer
Notebooks/journals of all sizes
Stapler and paperclips
File folders
Book shelves
Bottle of water
Kleenex
Scissors and Scotch tape

What about books? Do you have favorites close by? I have many poetry books: authors, anthologies, literary texts. Dictionaries, thesaurus, poetry manuals. My go-to poetry manuals are the heart-and-soul of my space. For example, I continuously refer to Frances Mays' *The Discovery of Poetry*. One is never so accomplished that prosody resources don't matter. I will always want and need all the help I can get. A big part of my bookshelf belongs to the *Princeton*

Encyclopedia of Poetry and Poetics (4th ed). What a gold mine of information. I also love the essays on the simplicity and complexity of poetry. If I am going to write the best I can possibly write, I want to ensure that my word choices, line composition, and overall language presence represent the best I can offer. You also need a handbook like Harbrace's *The Writer's Handbook*.

When I write about coal mining, or whisky drinking, or my hometown, it is necessary for me to speak with intelligence, emotion, and persuasion. If I am clear and convincing in my writing then I can be assured that my readers will not be left wondering.

Now, all of this goes back to the fundamental point of having the necessary space to do the necessary job of giving good writing. I look around my space and in its organized chaos I see the offerings of so many to help me.

How is your space working for you?

NOTES:

WHAT CATCHES US ON FIRE

Poetry As the Mechanism For Seeing Into the Life of Things

In all of my previous columns I have written about how poetry works, the role of language, mechanics, and how to start our own internalized fire for poetry. I've written about poetry as a way to witness current events or to watch nature. What do I mean by this topic? In my unfolding explanation down this page, I attempt not to be redundant, but to offer some new/different sight lines using poetry.

How does poetry work to see the necessary points of life… and death? I submit that the first work poetry has to do here is get our attention. This is best done by a powerful first line, especially if the poem is short. Say, ten lines, more or less. William Carlos Williams' poem, "The Red Wheelbarrow," is only eight lines containing sixteen words. But that first line, "so much depends," is a novel. This line is so expansive that it is amazing that it comes back to focus on the red wheelbarrow. That's how attention works.

Poetry asks us to move in all directions. Some critics would say poetry requires us to move. Either way the key is observation. We may see lots of things and we may need to make decisions about what to keep and what to discard. For example, you witness a bluebird singing and you see a nice-looking car drive by. That decision of what to keep and write about is likely pretty easy. But what if you witness an accident and you witness someone struggling with groceries. In that case you may want to keep both as writing potential. Observation is about choices.

Poetry is also about reaction times. I hinted at that above. How we may react quickly to an event, though the poem may take much longer to come together. We react, poetry reflects. The caveat to this, however, is speed. Today's electronic/digital age requires information to be sent at nanosecond speeds and read about as fast. There does not seem to be time to absorb the information and even to contemplate it. Poetry does not fit well with nanosecond speeds so this is why it could become a casualty. Spoken word poetry is one way to keep up as I see and hear young poets recite poetry in the fashion of hip-hop or rap.

Maybe poetry can be both things: Modern quick speed and slow thoughtful pacing. The quick one can relay immediate witness and the slower pace can provide perspective and documentary.

Lastly, poetry's vision can bring us all into solidarity… in the world… in all life.

Fire in Your Belly

Sometimes we want to write strongly about events or issues that particularly affect us. I get it. I often feel the same way. But here is the thing: How do really great poets and writers get their words across without coming across as "preachy"? The answer to that lies probably in what can be described as "poetic finesse." We can research about embracing the "great understanding" and how to write as a "witness," but what about the real fire that one feels. How do we harness that successfully into words and lines without failing our task?

Poets have always been viewed as having a passion for their writing. We see something, a minor thing, and we can create transformative verse that elevates our mind. If we are so lucky, the mind of the reader. Take the transformative poem, "The Red Wheelbarrow," by William Carlos Williams. His first two lines: "so much depends / upon…" You must agree those four words are transformative. Everything in our lives depends upon something or someone else, no matter how isolated we may be. I can sense Williams' "fire" in those few words because they speak to such large things out of his control.

Let's take that premise even further as we look at these opening lines from Lester Speiser: "Your violin shattered stars; / call yourself a nice Jewish / boy?" As the poem progresses I read Speiser getting more and more angry, but not at the boy (who ended up being a hero) but at the Nazis. The reading of this poem stirred in me an anger as well for the aftermath of the Holocaust.
This anger was that the Holocaust robbed so many of their lives and their futures. This poem showed me his "fire in the belly." That was his idea, I'm sure.

So, how do you channel this passion, this torch, these flaring embers into remarkable writing? First, look at word choices. Think of powerful words that can be chosen to make your points. Think of your senses. Which one (s) do you want to focus on? How you feel? What do you see? I often look to my surroundings to give me ideas/inspiration. A brightly-colored dolphin fish when in the water, and just hooked, is brilliant. But when it comes onto a boat, within seconds, it turns deathly grey. What an opportunity to use this as a metaphor. Elizabeth Bishop and others have used this same fish. Does "red" conjure up something deep within you?

Search for that fire, stoke it properly, with your creativity, then transform yourself while you transform others.

What Is It Really That We Want Poetry to Say?

In past columns I've discussed how poetry can lead us to a great understanding, can be a call to witness, and can lead us to appreciation of nature and humanity. But that is not all poetry needs to say. The poet Stanley Moss describes poetry as "a carnival of word play." I ask, how does poetry really come together and say something? We believe we have lots to say. We study forms, words, metrical patterns (or not), other poets, newspapers, and even other genres to give us help.

Here are some thoughts:

1. Slow down, and "smell the roses." If we rush through our writing, we may miss words and lines that require closer inspection. My work-out trainer constantly has to remind me to slow my movements, let my muscles feel the work. If we speed out the door, we could miss that charming bluebird.
2. Manage effectively your expectations. Start writing without thinking about winning a contest. Get it down. Then get it good.
3. Don't like what you've written? Before you throw it away, look through it and find at least one word or line that you do like. Put it down on a 3 x 5 card, save it for something else.
4. Manage distractions in your writing space. Set aside time. If you can't write, then at least read. Maybe read a poem you don't understand. Exercise your brain to dissect it until you find a meaning that satisfies you.
5. Free up your writing to find its own form. Truth be told, there is an organic process to what you write. It may show itself as a natural form to your poem. And if it comes together more like prose, then fine. You are seeking energy here.

We say what we say. We write what we write. Simple, yet complex. What we feel within us can stir us so magnificently that our writing becomes this unified strength. Here is something I included in my book, *Needville*:

Life and Death
My feet stay cold
in black water

like some blood's trickling
in hard rock veins

I'll die too young
to see my age

What will your poetry say to you, that you can say to your readers?

What Sparks Poetry?

I'm sure you've noticed that a long string of my columns has been more philosophical than based on poetry-writing mechanics. Poetry can be a mysterious genre in that we can learn all the rules (types of forms, like sonnets) which require adherence, then we can proceed to break them. We can argue that to be a true poet we must comply with the traditional, proven formal formats, if we choose to write that way. However, all of this gets turned over when modern experimental poetry arrives. Why I am discussing philosophy at this point is that I want to free poetry, give it noble purpose to liberate the world, heal all its wounds, and leave us with hope for now and in the future.

We must read poetry. Then we must read more poetry. We are seekers of poetic truth. As we pursue this we write as much as we can. Poetry is for everyone. In a recent article, I was amused to think that someone who is a famous chef might find interest in "A Short History of the Apple," by Dorianne Laux. Someone who enjoys the taste of distilled spirits might find pleasure in my poems about whisky, or those of Frank O'Hara.

Many notable and emerging poets have stated that the poems of Walt Whitman and T.S. Eliot sparked their way to writing. At the very least poetry has sparked an interest in reading, and not just poetry. In this same article I mentioned above, one person mentioned that a particular line from Mary Oliver's "Wild Geese" was a favorite: "You do not have to be good." Later in the same poem, "…the world offers itself to your imagination…" is as good advice as any poet could want.

Whether we write poetry as our response to climate change or as our response to personal heartbreak, we know we can count on other poets to help us gather our energy and expand our language. The first thing I do when I sit to write is read a few poems by my favorites and some new writers. A part of my joy is looking for that spark.

Be ready for when your sparks fly!

Can We Put Poetry to Good Use For Others?

What do I mean by that? I mean can we take poetry and help heal others, using the attributes of poetry. I recently read an essay in *Poets & Writers Magazine*, titled "Recovering Poetry." When I first saw this title, I thought it was about someone finding lost poetry. An archaeological dig exposing rare poetry treasures came immediately to mind. No, it wasn't about that at all. It was about something much more profound, and human: Using poetry to help someone overcome addiction. I read the essay with somber attention as it made me think about when I talk about writing "in the service of poetry." Why can't poetry also be in the service of others, a service of healing, more than that of a broken heart, but healing of a broken body?

For about ten years now I have been volunteering at an independent living retirement community. I lead a group discussing poetry appreciation by studying different poets or poetry topics each week. The average age of my group is about eighty-eight. They take notes in journals, ask terrific questions, and engage in discussions with me and each other. Two of the members have even published poetry books, for the first time in their lives. During the meetings members will talk about how the poems relate to their lives and how much they look forward to each week's meeting. I've been told that some have even experienced improved health and cognitive abilities.

In the essay I mentioned above the author talked about how some "coaches" used immersion workshops for clients in day treatments. Given poems to read, the participants were encouraged to write their own poems. The coaches emphasized focus by reading slowly and concentrating on words. It was clear to me that these workshops helped addicts transition back into the world they left. This time helped them find a better place with bodies and spirits on the mend.

Poetry as a great healer with its non-judgmental power. What a tribute to service.

Birdwatching: Poetry as Telescope Making

Taking my cue from Alix Oblin's essay on fiction writing, I thought how does watching birds simply being birds, assembly of a telescope, and creating poetry have anything in common. Bingo! Here goes my attempt to link all three:

The bird itself: First is a sighting, then close observation. See the details, such as feather composition, colors. Note the beak, the eyes, neck colors, tail feathers, shape of feet. Poets are known observers. When we see something new or different, the tendency is to know all we can about it.

Enter the telescope: the portal for close-up observation. How close do we want to be? Depends on the lens and scope length. When we select our telescope, we make a choice. How intimate to the subject do we want? That decision may determine our POV decision.

How about weight of the scope? Do we want it to be fixed or portable? This may influence how entrenched into the subject we will be. I prefer my scope to be portable so I can seize spontaneity. On a recent river cruise I used my camera's telescope function to bring in details of cathedral exteriors. I captured expressions on carvings I might have otherwise missed. Little bits of detail can tell a big story and later when I think back on my observations I can decide on words to describe my feelings.

At last, the poem: Here is where our finished scope and the subject come together to create a masterful poem. A classic example is W.H. Auden's *Musée des Beaux Arts*.
To the viewer Auden seems to be watching Icarus fall from the sky in Brueghel's famous painting, *The Fall of Icarus*. He

writes about what comes across as a seemingly ordinary event in which not even a farmer or passing ship notices. And this observation makes the poem all the more powerful.

So think about your images and thoughts as kinds of birds, all sorts, all colors. Your imagination is your lens and the completed scope your pen, moving back and forth, adjusting lines (your focus!). End result: A memorable poem.

Seen any unusual birds lately?

Energy: The High Bar for Poetry

Let's consider "energy." I don't mean do I have enough energy to write today, but the electrical charge that is our energy. All of the mechanics of poetry that we've learned come together, with our language, to form this "mass of energy" in our poetry. It's like the dark energy or dark matter of the universe. We can't see it, but we know it is there.

Here's my formula: **Imagination + Energy = Poem.**

I recently read an essay by poet Tess Gallagher. She starts her piece with this: "One outreaches language in poetry when the inseeing elements of consciousness ask the unseen of life to come forward." Note: The underlines I added. I kept re-reading that sentence until I concluded that "inseeing elements" were energy.

We know our poetry encompasses time and space. I've described dimension of poetry before but until this column I didn't discuss energy as one of the dimensions. To me, it is the same as the unseen energy that holds atoms together. Our energy is this "magical" force within our lines and words that holds verse together. This same energy imparts to us the totality of everything around us. Most of these things we write about: trees, waterfalls, butterflies, mountains, homeless people, iguanas. Each living or even inanimate subject of our writing carries its own energy, and if we are lucky as we study our subjects we tap into that energy.

Like Tess, we might see a brown moth "pressed like a pair of unpredictable lips" against a screen door. Feel that energy? Or we might be like William Carlos Williams who notes "The smell of the heat is boxwood/ when rousing us/ a movement of the air/ stirs our thoughts…"

There is energy in smell because it is unexpected but it has an impact. Another energy of heat can be when I think of my words "which/ smolder like/ forgotten live coals/ under a barely smoking fire pit." One of the laws of thermodynamics is that energy is neither created nor destroyed, only changed. That law applies to poetry, too.

Have you tapped into your energy sources lately?

Poetry as a Spiritual Exercise

We are aware that many poets, as their professional and personal lives expanded, felt that there was more to their writing than expressions on love, death, themselves, and nature. Many poets believed that they were on a quest, not just for truth, but for deeper meanings. For them, nature was a tool, a door, to allow them exploration into a spiritual side of their writing and consciousness.

Two notable poets, H.D. (Hilda Doolittle) and Robert Duncan spent a better part of their lifetimes into research on religion, and even the occult. They maintained "poetry affects spiritual transactions." For example, a devastating loss can compel one to seek solace in his/her faith then write about what this means to him/her. Edward Hirsch, an acclaimed poet, focuses much of his writing on traumatic events in his life. This includes elegies for family members and friends. The elegy can be a meditative reflection on sorrow, remorse, extreme anguish, which can be used in this form to heal. Edward lost his only son, Gabriel, and wrote a masterful 78-page elegy. In this he questions his faith, where God is, and even demanding that God give him back his son.

There were a number of poets of "the greatest age of English verse," who drew on *The Bible* as part of their prosody practice. We look to spiritual texts to give us inspiration as well as poetic technical help. For example, the meter, rhyme, and musicality of *The Bible* influenced many, such as John Donne and Walt Whitman. Our challenge today is to bring the antiquity to the present so that phrases continue to be relevant. Look at this line from Whitman (from his poem, "Memories of President Lincoln"):

> "I cease my song for thee, / From my gaze on thee in the west, fronting the west, communing with thee, / O comrade lustrous with silver face in the night…"

A poet incorporating spirituality in his renderings must find a balance between being pious and poetic.

Robert Alter's book, *"The Hebrew Bible: A Translation with Commentary"* looks discretely and intensely at biblical language and how to bring it to modern poetic script, as translation and as poetic thought. Take this example:

> "The Lord is my shepherd, / I shall not want. / In grass meadows He makes me lie down, / by quiet waters guides me. / My life He brings back. / He leads me on pathways of justice / for His name's sake. / Though I walk in the vale of death's shadow, / I fear no harm, / for You are with me."

When we use monosyllabic words with their modern syntax as we compose spiritual text, we create another kind of beauty.

How will you embrace spirituality in your writing?

The Purpose of the Evangelical Poet

Previously, I discussed what it meant to take a journey as a spiritual poet. Often in writing it can be difficult to separate the spiritual from the religious and from evangelism. But with evangelism defined more broadly we can give our writing a chance to take strong positions and use our verse to spread a more public view. Thus we connect with a larger audience and tap into a grander conscience.

I realize that for most of us writing on this scale could be unsettling, more risk than we want to take. But my purpose here is to show how vast poetry can be. It is your own choice to decide how large you want your writing to encompass. Not everyone can be a Walt Whitman, or a Richard Blanco. But there is plenty of room for big ideas as well as small ones. The essential change in our writing takes place when we write in the third person POV, the "we" replacing the "I." And unlike Blanco, we may not be called upon to write the ultimate public poem which was an evangelistic call to Americans. Look closely at this line, "All of us as vital as the one light we move through…", from his Inauguration (for Barack Obama) poem, "One Today." We hope to have words that enable us to write grandly of our lives, our country, and even our faith.

There are no more powerful metaphors for the strength of our emotions than those we find in nature. If we want our poetry to expand the public experience and draw society to us then using our love of nature is a natural choice. The mighty Sequoia doesn't just shade the tiny vole, it represents the strength and endurance of all of us. Wendell Berry ended his inspiring poem, "The peace of wild things," with this amazing line: "I rest in the grace of the world, and am free."

For those who believe in a higher power, it is the evidence of sunsets, shooting stars, trees blooming, baby animals, and the mysterious oceans. The ability to convey this as integral to the human experience is a type of evangelism. People and poetry, the perfect combination which gives us such a broad purpose. We have many chances to spread our verse.

Poetry, for better and for verse…

Poetry as Architecture: We Are Builders & Engineers

Have you thought of poetry composition as a three-dimensional structure? When we put words on paper, that is two-dimensional. But the technique of poetry composition incorporates more than ink and paper. We work on our technique or craft to give sounds, visuals, and textures. So, in practice, we add another dimension. Sometimes we place our writing in a certain period, a particular time. That's a dimension, too.

To anchor our structure, we rely on language. Think of the words as bricks, and our lines as the foundation we create from the bricks. What holds this together, then? What would you say is the mortar? I would say that use of space and punctuation would be good mortars. We have many options in the structure of our poem with use of space and commas. Please, no exclamation marks! They have all been used up; find another way to make our points or shout. Oscar Wilde, it was said, as an anecdote, labored all morning to add a comma, and then worked all afternoon removing it.

Much of the "dimensionality" of poetry rests on recitation, too. We hear poetry read out loud; we listen for the pauses that punctuation and spaces give us. These are part of the architecture.

Back to words. How do we build our poem? Do you have a special method or methods that prompt you to write? A journal is a good way to build a "writer's blueprint." I have a box I call my "Poetry Generator Machine." I made this after reading about Tristan Tarza and his Dada anti-establishment poetry movement. Look him up on Wikipedia. For my "machine" I cut out words from newspapers and magazines.

Throw them into this box. When I'm ready to write I put my hand in, rattle around the words, pull them out and place them on my desk. It's like Lego bricks. Sometimes this is how my architecture comes together. I like to think I'm a builder with words. I start the construction process, then lines form floors, and stanzas become stories. Don't you find it interesting that buildings in real life are described as having a "number of stories"?

We are writing engineers and literary constructionists. What will you build next?

Poetry & Philosophy

I know what you're thinking. I've gotten all lofty and grandiose. Please bear with me as I have some thoughts about how we get poetry to explain things. We want poetry to impart wisdom and knowledge, perhaps explain some universal truths. Perhaps we want to write about our own struggles to find meaning in life or answers (even before we know the questions). If we ask, why do I read poetry, one of the answers could be that poetry helps me understand my life.

Certainly "philosophy" is too vast and general a topic to write about here, but we can talk about poetry as one small part. We can use poetry to escape human limitations and take a worldly view of daily living. For instance, William Carlos Williams in his poem, "That is Just to Say," laments having eaten something being saved. But he is not apologetic as much as he is aware of his own satisfaction. So, the poem is about how one feels in doing something perhaps a little sneaky. No risk, no gain. Sometimes those four words describe the essence of writing poetry. Do we dare take on our language and push it to the limits? I've described imagination before, and if our knowledge is a part of our imagination then we form a philosophy of our poetry.

It is important to me that I have a mission in writing poetry. This mission doesn't have to be complicated, but it should be purposeful. Even writing simple poems destined for light reading have a purpose. Poems delving into deep topics of faith draw upon our acquired wisdom. Wallace Stevens wrote: " There are levels of thought or vision where everything is poetic." And there are even examples of poetry where nothing is poetic. Writing about war and suffering is not one's typical "poetic" topic, but nonetheless the rendering of words and lines are constructed as poetry. The Ukrainian-American poet, Ilya Kaminsky is a master of this:

> "That was the summer we damned only the earth. /
> That was the summer strange helicopters circled."

Our personal philosophy evolved from our continuing education of life around us. We take images of everything we see, sounds of what we hear, sensory pleasures of what we taste and touch. These help us create our language. We then give this to readers and with these gifts we understand our purpose as poets.

Why Do We Care About How Poems Come About?

I recently received the poetry book, *Brute* (Winner of the 2018 Walt Whitman award), by Emily Skaja. This manuscript of some thirty poems almost stands as one long poem. The book is about a relationship, and not a really good one. There are many passages in there that could be universal to many women, for instance. So it becomes relatable. When a poet writes about personal experiences, the context is less clinical and more emotional. Having said that, we may not be as interested in all the details of emotional experiences of the writer that led to the work, as we are in the quality of the poems.

We look for intention and then beyond that meaning. For with those two aspects we can gather what appeals to the reader. Now as writers we don't want to burden our readers with deep background of ourselves. For one thing they may not even care, and for another, how could we select which were instrumental in the creation of our poetry. Our business is to write compelling poetry and theirs is to be moved or inspired.

We use the words we've been collecting in our personal "poetry generator machine," to give us the settings, be they of tone, place, or time. These are the dimensions of poetry and while we fixate on tying all of these together, we let our imaginations and our experiences add the dimension of depth. Recall that I have touched on these in past columns. So, how do our poems come about? Poet A.E. Housman generally composed his poems during afternoon walks. Relaxed and maybe a little drowsy from his lunch, his mind was free to wander among the weeds and hills. Sometimes our poems are spontaneous, jumping out of a lake, or a glass of whisky.

While I don't know if the poems in *Brute* were spontaneous, I have to believe they evolved from intense emotional pain and disappointments. So maybe her intentions were to heal herself and then this collection came about to share the meanings she found.

When poems come about, from whatever source, we see the service to poetry. How do you see your service? Do you have a "muse" or particular inspiration that primes your writing pump?

As you continue the path that is your writing, I hope you will be inspired by one person who I found quite philosophical, Yogi Berra. " When you get to the fork in the road, take it."

Why Do We Envy Other Poets?

Oh, that suspicious little word comes creeping into our heads: envy. We find ourselves caught up in this emotion at conferences, workshops, or even readings. What is it about exposure to the success of others that creates an uncomfortable feeling of inadequacy?

We don't serve poetry or ourselves when we let ourselves slip into this. Think of the wasted energy when you could have studied the "competition" and learned some things. I use the word, "competition," because like other writing genres, poetry is not immune to the effects of competitive situations. We know that there are many many writers and a limited number of awards, grants, publications. We also know that there are likely more writers than readers, so that intensifies the anxiety.

We all fall into the same trap of envy, but the key to our own success is understanding more about ourselves and our writing expectations. For example, I would love to see one of my poems published in a major literary journal. But is that what defines me as a successful writer? Sure we all want to sell our books, the more the better, we think. To whom? How many people would have to buy our books for us to feel like we are successful? If we don't sell our works like we thought we would, does that make us less a writer? Perfect breeding grounds for envy!

I love to write and I feel a keen sense of accomplishment when something I have penned makes me feel good. I don't want to find myself blocked by inadequacies of my own creation. I didn't start writing poetry because I had visions of greatness and huge prizes. Neither did Anne Sexton start writing poetry for that. Her doctor suggested she write as a means of dealing with her mental illness. Sometimes it is simply fate that brings attention and fame to writers.

We poets are solitary workers of our craft. And we know that gratification exists in the compositions we create. This brings me back to an essential question: What do *YOU* want from your writing? Are you satisfied with your essential writing self? I hope so because if not you may be robbing yourself, and possibly others, of a magical part of your existence.

What Is the Worth of My Writing?

There come times when we question the value of our writing. Not necessarily an economic question, but the figurative esoteric value. It is one of the eternal doubts that all writers face. I think poets have a double-dose of it, however, because our market is smaller than the other genres; and the brevity, with which we generally write, creates a closer scrutiny. For example, I give myself permission to quit a book if, after about forty-five pages, the writing is not doing it for me. I have attached a value to this, and the value is my time. With poetry, the timeline is very short for me. If I don't "get it," after the first few lines, I am done.

This brings up the question I have based on my own personal writing history: How do I overcome self-doubts, such as fear I am not good enough, or others think I'm not. In previous columns I've addressed things like for whom do we write, envy of others, and how do we keep the creativity river flowing. At the end of the day this poetry writing stuff really boils down to your own personal perception of you. If you truly believe in yourself then ultimately you will get there. Why is that? Well, your own desire to be a good writer for your personal internal critic will compel you to expand your language, to focus on forms that fit your style, and to give you satisfaction.

What would happen if you gave one of your poems to two respected poets who you may casually know, and asked for their opinions? What if they responded and disagreed on whether your poem was good? Who would you believe? Think about how subjective poetry is. What if you took a poem of a well-known poet, gave it to these same two, and they had the same disagreement? What then? In both cases the works were worthy. Because readers have a difference of opinion doesn't mean anything more than that, a difference.

We are not striving for perfection to prove worth, are we? As William Carlos Williams wrote in a poem, "There are no perfect waves— / Your writings are a sea…"

Cast off your doubts; simply write.

Humorous Poetry

I have written about the cultures and ideas of poetry, but have yet to discuss a lighter form: humor, an essential topic for poetry. I am not talking about limericks, puns, or cowboy poetry doggerel, but the type of humorous poetry whose principal role is make the reader smile. Who writes that? For starters, Billy Collins and Garrison Keillor come to mind for modern day writers. Even back in the early centuries of poetry there has been much "lighter-hearted" compositions. Think Shakespeare as the quintessential reference.

But let's discuss modern times. How can we persuade our reading public that poets can be funny, amusing, memorable in a "smiley" kind of way? We can try adventurous rhymes, heavy alliteration, bizarre visuals, and tongue-in-cheek wordsmithing. In fact, we can gain readers' attention with a book title like *The Rain in Portugal* by Billy Collins. He has a poem in there, "On Rhyme," which pokes fun at the old rhyme scheme for remembering which months have thirty days or where in Spain rain pours. But this poem has no rhyme to it! This poem is really a lighter approach to a wonderful memory he had about a trip. Another poet, Patrick Chewning, has a chapbook, *Chicken-Fried Escargot*. What a title, right? His poem, "Priorities," from this book, speaks to his love of fishing and his love of writing poetry. I love this line: "If someone doesn't like your fish poem, he probably can't fish." When we talk of love of nature and can see humor and humanity in it, then we are offering up a great connection.

One of my favorites, Nikki Giovanni, in her poem: "Letting the Air Out (of my tires)" offers right at the start:
  "This is not / a country song // I am not / a dixie chick /..."

I am smiling at this point because I know she is going to make a big point later in the piece.
And she delivers eloquently on how the humanness of us all makes us forgive and move on, appreciating the frailty of mankind.

So humor in our poetry can give us an opportunity to present strong messages in a less intimidating and serious way. Smile, this is only a movie.

What is Poetry, & Does This Count as It?

Taking my cue from a recent article in *The New Yorker*, I thought I might offer up a lighter look at *Poetry Matters*. I do this because I've often heard (too often, I fear) that poets don't have a sense of humor. Try telling that to Billy Collins. And see my previous column on humorous poetry. But here is another approach. In 2022 what is poetry?

Let's think about this and come up with a realistic list of what we think comprises poetry in this year:
1. Do we still need pencils to write poetry? Is it only poetry if we use pencils?
2. Do lines composed on a laptop count as composing poetry?
3. When writing about serious events, does a poet have to spill real blood?
4. If a poet clips her nails while writing, does that count as invoking her muse?
5. Do you have to have a band-aid on your left eyebrow that has *shit* spelled on it in order to prove you are a real writer?
6. Does your writing space have to have real books in it or can you supply it with fake ones so visitors to the space will say, "Ah, you are a real writer."
7. If you are not writing poetry, can you simply sit at a Starbucks with a notebook and iPhone, strike a literary pose, and pretend you are creating a sonnet about baristas?
8. Can you spill coffee or sweetened iced tea on a few pages of doodles, show it to a neighbor, and say, "I was working on my best poem yet, when the doorbell rang, and broke my concentration"?
9. Do you think everyone you know actually knows more about poetry than you?

10. If so, don't let them know that. Pretend, if you have to, to know more about poetry than anyone.
11. If you have not been invited lately to give a reading, create your own reading event. Email everyone you know and a lot you don't. People often come to readings so everyone can see them, not necessarily to hear or see you.

Above all else, keep writing. Buy a few real poetry books. Read them. Get some pencils.

Normal Size of a Poem

What is the "normal" size of a poem (see column on Epic Poetry)? Is there a "calibration standard" for poetry length? We don't use calipers or carpenter squares to measure length on a page. That is too left-brain for us creative types. But we do study and investigate words to ponder over stresses, syllables, and metrical formats, especially if we are writing formally (i.e. sonnets). Many of us contemporary poets embrace free verse style so we think about compression and compaction when we compose. We edit a lot, revise a bunch, and throw away words that we decide will be unnecessary or even lazy.

Getting the words down, then getting them good is our faithful mantra. This also means words play a major role in length. The novelist Greg Iles says he writes "in a granular way," meaning his descriptions often unfold minute-by-minute. That's why most of his novels are long and epic. I love his writing. Poet C.D. Wright was one of many writers who composed "verse novels" using topics, such as civil rights, to engage her readers. Her verse-book, *One With Others*, is a testament to how incorporation of letters, lists, reporting, comes together as poetry. To tackle a big heavy topic such as civil rights, she needed to be different, and she succeeded.

While we may not have something that large inside us, we still have plenty of space to occupy between a great length and a few lines. What we strive for is that at the end of the last line of the last stanza our readers are left wanting more.

Here is William Carlos Williams' "The Manoeuvre":

"I saw the two starlings
coming in toward the wires.
But at the last,
Just before alighting, they

turned in the air together
 and landed backwards!
that's what got me— to
face into the wind's teeth."

Every word counts in what is a normal-size poem for you. The big can be seen in the small. Face the wind, and pull your words out of clouds.

LET'S GET MECHANICAL

The Voice of Poetry

There are several elements that compose a poem. These are considered the basic mechanicals, and are often described as voice, images, lines, forms, words and movement.

In this essay, I want to talk about what I consider the most noticeable part of a poem, when first read: The voice. Without thinking about it too deeply, when we read a poem for the first time, we often notice in what "person" the poem is written. Very frequently, poems are "I" poems. If we go back to our nostalgic memories of poetry, we can recollect our exposure to Emily Dickinson and Walt Whitman. These two were considered latter day and even close to modern poets. We all learned lines of Edgar Allan Poe, Robert Browning, Percy Shelley, and Shakespeare. Among the things they had in common, was the frequent narration in the first person. From Robert Browning's, "I send my heart up to there, all my heart / In this my singing…" to Emily Dickenson's "I died for Beauty — but was scarce…" we were drawn into the personal experience of the poet in composing the poem. And that is what "I" poems do. They bring the reader right into the middle of the dialogue or the action.

Today's modern poets differ in most part by taking the strict poetic forms (and we'll get to those in another column) out of the context and focusing on the message. They want their voices to be heard and their message absorbed through our very skins. We see the voice of the poem and we determine (sometimes unaware) what the tone of the poem is from this perspective. The voice, in other words, will determine if the tone is friendly, intimidating, sad, contemplative, or angry.

When we get into the poem and see which voice is active, we can learn who the speaker of the poem is and who the listener is. We might see that the listener may be a third party that the writer (or narrator) is addressing. Will we identify then with the listener or with the writer? Often I think that is one of the enjoyable parts of reading poetry. Who do you think that Robert Frost was addressing when he wrote these lines in his poem "The Sound of Trees":

> "I wonder about the trees /Why do we wish to bear / Forever the noise of these /More than another noise… //"

If we read further into the poem, he continues in the first person, but the tone is reflective. He's thinking about how important trees are to him. And I feel like he is talking to me and that I (his reader) am to whom he is addressing the poem. So, as the listener, I become very interested in what he is saying. This poem is very effective on a number of levels.

One of the most effective practitioners of voice in her poetry was Anne Sexton. She was part of a group of poets known as the "confessional" poets. A major characteristic of the writing of this group was their use of personal revelations. Ms. Sexton actually began writing poetry at the suggestion of her psychiatrist for part of her therapy. She had suffered a number of mental breakdowns, and for all her life was plagued by her own personal demons. She was charismatic, unpredictable, and her voice was described as "flamboyant and searing." Her major themes were her sanity and her womanhood challenges. Her poem, "Her Kind,"is the one she often started her public poetry readings with. The first lines go:

> "I have gone out, a possessed witch, /haunting the black air, braver at night; /dreaming evil, I have done my hitch …// Then she ends the poem with: A woman like that is not ashamed to die. / I have been her kind."

Even with these small samples of her writing, we are drawn into the power of the poem. This, too, is an excellent poetic rendering from a master of verse.

The voice and tone of a poem, when they work, make us such a part of the reading experience that we want to read more of that particular poet. We are not intimidated by their writing, we are fascinated by it. And we find we want more.

So, I encourage you to pick up some classical poetry and some modern ones, then look first to whom the poem is presented. Try to visualize for whom the poem is written and how the voice is coming across. As we pursue other mechanics of the poem in future columns, the goal will be to see how we can enrich the entire poetic experience.

Until then, I leave you with another few lines from Anne Sexton's poem, "The Room of My Life":

> "Here/in the room of my life /the objects keep changing...//
> ...I feel the world in here too, /offering the desk puppy biscuits. / However, nothing is just what it seems to be. / My objects dream and wear new costumes,...//"

Lines of Poetry, Part I

As we continue through the mechanics of poetry composition, the structure of lines of our verse becomes very important. Our words start to form in an organized way and we want to create a structure which is probably one of the most important elements of our composition. Taking time to properly format our lines can yield powerful verse as well as provide notable attention to the poet's voice.

Here are some observations to consider when constructing your lines:

*Do you want the line to be taut or concise? Or do you want it be free-flowing, loose, wordy? One of the best poets to use taut lines and precise wording is Kay Ryan. Check out how she carefully places her words in any of her books.

*How will you select your end words? Do you want your reader to linger at the end of each line, or move quickly to the next? Remember: the last word always gets attention.

*When looking at each side of your poem, can each side be equally strong? Imagine a line right down through the middle of your stanza. How does each side of it look?

*Do you want your lines to end-stop or run over to the next line, or even the next stanza?

*Looking back at the beginning of your poem, how does it start? Immediately? Or do you lead your reader into a build-up of action?

*Does the poem end abruptly? How do you want it to end?

*In looking over your completed poem, how do you think it comes across? Overstated? Understated?

*Are your lines consistent in length, or do you have variation between short and long lines in differing stanzas? How do you think this works, or not?

*Checking back on your line punctuation, did you use any? Why, or why not? If you select to use punctuation, which according to poet Dana Gioia, is your friend, make sure you are using commas and periods (and other forms) correctly.

*How do you want to present "pauses" in your lines? Study the poetry of Rae Armantrout for excellent examples of well-placed words, lines, and spaces.

Line strength is a remarkable poetic characteristic that can lead you and your readers further into the beauty and magic of your writing. This can be one of the best ways to tap into your creativity.

Are you ready to get in line?

Lines of Poetry, Part II

Before I move on to other mechanics of poetry, I'm spending a little more writing space in this column for lines. The practical reason is that this mechanic is so important that I don't want to short change it for you. So much of what we've been reading so far in this column comes to fruition in the line. In fact, we couldn't do or say what we want to in composing poetry if it were not for the strength of our lines.

James Longenbach has devoted an entire book, *The Art of the Poetic Line* (Graywolf Press), on the necessity of mastering the poetic line. In fact, he starts right off in the Preface saying, "Poetry is the sound of language organized in lines." Line is what defines the writing of poetry and separates poetry from the other genres. Even within music, when we hear lyrics that particularly touch us, we generally recall them by saying, "what a great line that was." Everything that is written is defined by lines, but in poetry we recognize there is a certain rhythm, a certain expectation, and anticipation, that is conveyed by the careful placement and content of lines.

One of the most important components of line is syntax. Strictly speaking, syntax is the organization of words in a sentence (or line!) with a particular relationship. Within poetry composition, we arrange our words in lines with particular breaks, punctuation, pauses, and endings. The careful use of "breaks" can lend drama to a well-crafted poem. But we need to be careful we retain the integrity of the poem itself. When we are creating very strict poetic compositions, we need to pay special attention to words and syllables and the proper incorporation of meter. Shakespeare is the expert in this area.

In contemporary and modern poetry, we may swerve away from rhyming, and to some sense metrical poise, but nonetheless we need to stay close to syntax and the ways to end our lines and stanzas. Breaks and enjambments become very important and are major parts of developing the flow of the poem. Look closely at the poetry of Marianne Moore, Elizabeth Bishop, T.S. Eliot, and Ezra Pound. These four, in my opinion, were at the forefront of contemporary poetry as it evolved from 19th century practice to that of the 20th century. While they may have liberated much of their poetry from stricter forms, they retained all the basics and their free verse is all the richer for it. Here's an example from Marianne Moore's poem, "To Military Progress":

    "You use your mind
    Like a millstone to grind
      Chaff…"

Until next time…

Form & the Work of the Poem

In previous columns, I have written on the mechanics of poetry, such as movement, lines, voice and image. I'll soon cover words; in this column I talk about "form." If I confine my comments to contemporary poetry, I don't give justice to the formal aspects of poetry composition. I'm referring to the pre-20th century writings that existed before Walt Whitman and others like him. We all remember, and many of us still write poetry in the romantic styles or those of 18th and 19th century where meter, rhyming, strict syllable count, and style forms (i.e. sonnet, villanelle, sestina, blank verse, etc.) were the driving forces. I suggest that if you want to write in the strict poetic forms that you study them in great depth and practice writing them a lot.

In contemporary poetry, and in the post-modern eras of poetry, we see free verse, prose verse, what I call "scatter" verse (see Douglas Kearney's "Noah/Ham: Fathers of the Year") and "free-form composition" verse (see John Hollander's "Swan and Shadow"). To me, poetry writing today is all about taking risks with form. Some writers even say, the riskier the better. I don't know if I agree with going all out. Poetry still has to make sense; it still must reveal truths and ideas. Even if I play with form, I still want the reader to receive the poem's message.

So, here are some considerations when it comes to your poem's form:

*What does the poem's shape say about the subject of the poem?

*In composing the lines, does each start with a capital letter? Why?

*Are the lines irregularly placed? Does this work for the poem?

*How are the stanzas constructed? How are you using white space?

*If using rhymes, are they forced or do they work for the poem?

*A powerful construct is repetitive lines or words. Does the repetition emphasize or detract?

*Do you want to use a metrical pattern?

*Does the use of punctuation help or hinder the form?

Whether we are writing a prose poem or a strictly "formal" piece, all of the mechanics we have talked about come together to provide the narrative. Our word choices again will play a most important role. One poem I particularly like is Forrest Gander's "Sinister." He varies the stanza lengths, gives some specific visuals, uses articles in productive ways, and then keeps the flow moving to a successful ending. Another way to progress a poem, especially a long one, is to use section breaks as part of the form. In my poem, "Just This Once, Another Once," (from *Stones for Words*), I used Roman numerals to separate the dream sequences to keep the narrative moving forward. My form was narrow free verse with variable stanza lengths using haikus inserted as pauses.

Think about your poem's form and give shape to your message. Take risks.

The Movement of Poetry

With traditional poetic forms, we have relied on metrical configuration to create the rhythm and movement. Even in free verse, there is a rhythm created by words, rises and falls of phrases or lines, and the flow of stanzas. For example: Are we writing the activity using passive or active verbs? How does our choice affect the movement forward of the poem? Are the tenses consistent?

Just thinking about the choice of verbs enables us to bring the reader into our story, or narrative, if you will. When we set about to develop the poem itself, we will decide if we want to tell a personal story; present an argument, perhaps of a political tone; or describe some natural occurrence or scene. We can look into our personal poetry craft box and choose among the many craft implements to get us going. As we line up words for images and the voice, we know we have to assemble our "story" and within this we know we will want to see the poem unfold in some type of logical progression, or movement. To me, creating the activity by selecting verbs is one of the more enjoyable processes in creating poetry.

Putting the words in motion and using them in lines that propel the poem in a forward direction is challenging and fun. Do I want to use verbs to flashback as a movement? Do I want to select verbs that create a flashforward leap to the future? How will I line up my poem to best convey either direction?

I must take care to ensure my poem stays on track and with the subject as well. I can stray or lose my way within the poem; or I'll take both the reader and myself off course. I have to remember that my writing must be concise, economical. It is tempting to create long lines thinking that this will enable the story or narrative to have greater impact. Consider, however, what you may give up by doing so. You will give up the chance for the reader to do some pleasant work along with you. Compare and contrast William Penn Warren and W.H. Auden. I study them both to understand compromise of line length, rhythm, and creating a magical poem. While they were contemporaries, both were masters of the movement of poetry and both created this in totally different ways. Movement and form are tied together and W.H. Auden shows us how creative we can be with both.

Then take into consideration the poetry of Denise Levertov. One excerpt from her poem, "The Wanderer," is quite succinct:

> "He has taken his sorrow / away to strangers. /They form a circle around it, / listening, touching, / drawing it forth."

That's movement and rhythm. See, poetry relies on physics, too!

Are you moving?

The Image in Poetry

As poets, we bring to readers our particular experiences, thoughts, hopes, troubles, and just about everything else regarding life. We want to draw our readers into our minds and hearts gaining either their empathy, or pulling them into our illusions. Our motivations are what make poetry magical and compelling. One of the most effective ways we can have our poetry make great impact is through imagery. As the poem comes together, as the lines and words are initialized, the poet enriches the craft by considering:

* The senses. Do you want to evoke them? If so, how many and what are they?
* Effective imagery. How do the details form your "poetic picture"? Look at the poems of Marianne Moore, Sylvia Plath, Amy Clampitt, and William Carlos Williams.
* Immediacy of the poem. Does it exist, or is it distant?
* How is the poem viewed? Picture a telescope and choose from which end you want the reader to see. What effect do you want this to have?

When we create mental pictures, we create the imagery. While sight is the most obvious sense, the others are not ignored. Mastery of the poem succeeds when the reader is brought totally within the poem's scene. We long for our readers to become immersed so much that without even knowing it at first, they find they can hear, smell, touch, and even taste what is written there. The subtlety of the words can conjure up images that provide the desired tension as well as the desired satisfaction.

As you start the writing process, when you are selecting your words, allowing your imagination and experiences to take shape, consider words that are interesting, solid, and specific. Words that have a texture, not only on paper, but on the tongue, can provide the good image that is more than just a mere description. For example, words like *husks, thistle, marsh, plush, flute,* and *davenport.* Look for word combinations that can be visualized, even though you might not be able to see them. In her poem, "An Old Whorehouse," Mary Oliver, with these simple lines, opens us up to our senses:

"spiders had wrapped up / the crystal chandelier."

William Carlos Williams from his poem, "The Woodthrush," offers us:

"his dappled breast reflecting / tragic winter / thoughts my love my own"

Let your words suggest pictures of the mind. Don't be timid about throwing into your writing vividness from your dreams, your trips to the local grocery, or by simply sitting quietly and free-associating. Study photographs or take a trip to a museum and jot down impressions of the senses that you feel.

Wanted: Words, Alive-Not Dead, Part I

This column will be in two parts as words require that much attention. In past columns on Language, Concreteness and Abstraction I've discussed words in larger concepts. However, I can never overstate the importance of words. The definition of a poem: An arrangement of words in verse. While these words may be more powerful than words used in ordinary speech, there still are some basic concepts for consideration.

Let's start with this: English is essentially two languages. One is our everyday vernacular, ordinary words, mostly spoken. The second is the written where words are more complex and whose main purpose is to state facts with precision and accuracy. So when we embark on our poetry journey we consider what we want our English to be or do. Do we want our words to showcase our intelligence and serve our egos? Or do we want to be more relaxed and perhaps more genuine. In this latter consideration we tend to be more interesting, therefore our writing will show this. We want our poetry to avoid being described as stuffy or inaccessible. Poetry is perfect for expressing our ideas and passions in simpler formats with shorter, more familiar words. This is clarity.

Bear in mind that the reader or listener is interested in what you have to say. So, the more of "you" that is found in your word choices, the more interesting your writing becomes. For example, as you write, would you find the word "negligent" as accessible as "careless?" We see the stuffy, "forthwith," not as modern as "now." Try this for comparison: "I long for the heat of your touch, it is sufficient to keep me." to "I long for the heat of your touch, it is enough." See how I present words that stand a better chance of making it in poetry? The reader gets the joy of interpreting what is enough.

There really is no reason as we construct our poems to use more complex words when the simple ones will work just as hard, if not harder, to win our readers. In simple words, we can engage our readers without robbing the language of creativity.

Next column: How do we make our words come alive?

Wanted: Words, Alive-Not Dead, Part II

As a continuation of my previous column, I draw on Greg Orr's chapter, "Words Coming Alive in Poems," from his book, *A Primer For Poets*. He states: "[p]oets are fascinated by what words can do when arranged into certain patterns…" It's not that we are "manipulators" of language, as much as we are enthralled by words and their potential magic. In my poem, "Wasting Metaphors," I likened the poem to a long-simmering roast in a slow cooker where the words simmered, and I could then peer in and be shocked. Not to confuse you; but, I'm not saying that poets follow a recipe or an organic chemistry text to write. What I am saying is that in the selection of words, we carefully decide what works. See what one critic says about Emily Dickinson:

"Dickinson's poetry is notable for its peculiar agrammaticality: unexpected plurals, inverted syntax, and an often complete disregard for gender, person, or agreement between nouns and verbs." (from Ana Luisa Amaral in *The Literary Hub*). An example is from her poem, number 276:
> "Many a phrase has the English language— Low as the laughter of the Cricket."

Here she takes an insect and gives it a voice we can hear and understand within the context of her poem.

Often to make our poetic points we take inanimate objects and give them a metaphorical life. In a sense this creates a new word for our purposes. This "new word" may serve several purposes, such as offering sound as well as a new use. In Joy Harjo's poem, "Once the World Was Perfect," she takes a feeling word (doubt) and gives it new purpose:

"...Then Doubt pushed through with its spiked head."

What a terrific way to give body to a feeling. We all can connect or relate to feelings of doubt; but when we give it "gut" strength then we are going well beyond just skepticism. We are so immersed with the thought that something like doubt could be so powerful, it simply hurts.

Think about your words, create and continually add to your "poetic dictionary," with your words as hammers/mallets/brushes and your pages as nails/pegs/canvas.

Metaphor & Simile

In creating images within our poetry, we can incorporate "poetry-proven" expressions, such as metaphor and simile, which bring dramatic focus to our words. Both of these can work to achieve the same effect, but in different ways. Technically, metaphor and simile are *tropes*, or figurative expressions. By using words or phrases in such a way that their normal use is taken out of its usual context and placed into another, new meanings can arise. In other words, the poet, in composing an image for the reader, can choose words or phrases which give meaning on one level; and at the same time, give another completely different meaning. Metaphors rely on images; similes rely on comparison, often with the use of "like" or "as."

By incorporating metaphor or simile, the poet gives the poem greater depth, dignity, mystery, and persuasion, leading to even more enjoyment of the writing. A grand example of a great metaphoric poem is Maxine Kumin's "Woodchuck." In this seemingly harmless nature poem, she describes the travails of dealing with pesky woodchucks in her garden. She has the reader rocking along amused at her various efforts at eradication, until the reader reaches the last lines. Then we see what the poem is really about. She's writing about how the Jews were exterminated by the Nazis. Her power is her subtlety. Another excellent poet, Billy Collins, is a master of metaphor as well. One example that I really am fond of is his poem, "Litany." Many writers turn to Sylvia Plath for examples of metaphor, and I would certainly suggest reading her poetry. Her symbolism is based on graphic images and powerful language. "Gleaming with the mouths of corpses," is one of her best lines.

Two other poets known for simile are Robert Frost and Anne Sexton. If, as a writer, you create the image using "like" or "as" in very unorthodox ways, you will hook in your reader. Take this image, from Anne Sexton's poem, "The Abortion:"

> "… The road was as flat as a sheet of tin."

Here is another one, from "Rowing:"

> "… I was stamped out like a Plymouth fender…"

Robert Frost, whose poetry captures all the essences of nature, uses both simile and metaphor for how man relates to nature. His social commentaries can be found in some of his simplest poems, all the better because of his word choices. For instance, in "The Silken Tent," he connects us with earth by starting out:

> "She is as in a field a silken tent / At midday when a sunny summer breeze / Has dried the dew and all its ropes relent…"

When you can put together your lines with carefully chosen words, like Rick Barot uses in one of his poems, "leaves hanging down like green bats from the branches," and "sheet cakes of snow on top of cars," then you are well on your way to masterful, imaginative, and evocative poetry. The words don't have to be big; they simply have to be placed in a creative context.

Words & Poetry

We've looked at lines; we've reviewed metaphor and simile; we've considered imagery; and we've talked about the shape of the poem. We looked at word choices. But how do we choose our words? We know we want to practice quality over quantity; but, we also believe that all the good words have not been used up. Or have they?

How do we avoid overusing words? It would be so easy to grab onto a cliché to make our poetic points. We don't want to do that. We want our words to be fresh, concrete, absolute, vague, mysterious, sensuous. Contrasting and comparing using unique wording gives us a wide range of creativity options. For instance, if your hands could "feel" the surface of sounds that your words make, how would these words feel? Giving depth and texture to writing is part of the magic that good poets have.

Suppose you are writing a poem about the sea. What poet hasn't? How would you describe it in such a way that would be novel? Waves hitting the shore could be unraveling their secrets and just when we approach them they pull back leaving us wondering what it was they had. Could you describe layers of the water as it moves from surface through the depths? How would these layers feel to you? Frigid, icy, bone-jarring, breath-stopping, heel-biting? Imagination can be at the heart of word choices. Imagine writing the sea poem with crayons instead of a pen.

One of the many reasons that Billy Collins is so popular is his ability to take even the simplest words and create minor masterpieces with them. Again using his poem, "Litany," he gives us a love poem where the subject is "the bread and the knife, the crystal goblet and the wine." He continues with a number of comparisons and contrasts using plain words, nothing flowery or showy at all. Yet his poem vibrates with the intensity of "the sound of rain on the roof." This is a terrific poem.

Another favorite wordsmith is Louise Glück. She writes of disappointments and frustrations in love and relationships, for the most part. She starts out in "Celestial Music," with this simple line: "I have a friend who still believes in heaven." Small words setting up a really big image. This poem moves in a conversational way and this is a novel approach, too. I love how some poets can take internal and external conversations and create wonderful verse. In "Siren," she sets us up for another relationship conflict by giving us these first two lines:

> "I became a criminal when I fell in love. / Before that I was a waitress."

Again, simple words, huge premise.

In the next column, I'll continue with words discussion… our language.

Language & Poetry

In this second column on the subject of words and their choices, I talk about "language," or as I like to think of it, "how our words speak to and for us." When we talk about other cultures' native tongues, we refer to them as their language: an alphabet that has been used to form words, which strung together become a language.

Poets take language and fashion it in such ways as to give the best use of their word choices. I used in the previous column examples from two of my favorite poets, Billy Collins and Louise Glück. There is a group of poets known as the "language poets." Why would they be categorized as such? Well, for starters, one reason is they are considered by their contemporaries so proficient in their wording and composure. They have distinguished themselves. An excellent example of one of the best known language poets is Rae Armantrout. In 2010, she won the Pulitzer Prize for poetry with her book, *Versed*. Her poems are notable not just for language with the everyday syntax she uses, but for how she forms the actual poems. Some lines may have only one or two words, and with that she gives strong positioning. From her poem, "Pleasure," in the book, look at these lines:

> "A sleight-of-hand / equilibrium / being produced / as bees / pass one another, / a ticklish rumble / shuttling between blooms. / I'd like to think / I'm one, / no, / all of them...//"

When we select our words, we like to think we have some special end in mind. For instance, the word "reptile" might mean many things at first read. But I'm just planting the seed here. You may not know what I am thinking or planning to do with that word. I could be thinking of a young orange-tinted box turtle grazing in my flowerbed; or I could be thinking of a copperhead snake sleeping on top of our wood pile. You might think these two examples are something cute and something repulsive or scary. Language is the art of words, their definitions, and their connotations. The artistry of the poet comes to the forefront when he or she picks carefully through words and assembles poetic language.

Could you create a poem that describes the beauty of a venomous snake taking a nap in the shade of a lilac bush, for instance? What about the symbolism of the hour-glass pattern on the copperhead's skin? Can it be described as magical?

How will you form your language? Can you see your poetry evolving in unique and wonderful ways, digressing from the traditional poetic modes into other expressive conveyances?

In a separate column, I talk about how concreteness and abstraction work best for the poet. The common creative writing advice, "show, don't tell," applies to poets as well as to the other genre writers.

The Definite in the Indefinite

What is the aim of poetry? Is one of its intents to use words to mean many things? Does poetry take the complexity of things around us and reduce them to the smallest number of words, in hopes that some logic, or definition, remains?

As poets we look at the abstract and make it concrete. And we take the concrete and make it abstract. Our craft may evolve from the choice we make. While some writers may propose that poetry is "slipperier" than the other genres, I propose that when we choose our words, form our lines, and complete our craft, we have taken complexity, reduced it to its basic atomic structure, and given it an interesting worth. For example, William Carlos Williams and A.R. Ammons have taken two very short poems, "The Red Wheelbarrow" and "Reflective," respectively, and opened up ambiguity so much that we actually can derive meaning from these poems. Further, Williams even offers us a solution to the motion of words in his poem, "The Poem," with the lines: "It's all in / the sound. A song." We can appreciate that poetry has motion just like music. He concludes that poem with the words, "centrifugal, centripedal." These two words also sum up the workings of poetry. Isn't it interesting that he may be the only poet who has put these two words in a poem?

Does good poetry writing strive for an ambiguity, creating an endless search for meaning? One critic described this as "lemon squeezing." I think of it more like peeling the shell off a hard-boiled egg. Sometimes the shell comes off in just a few large pieces, other times it seems I have to wrench the shell off in many tiny fragments bringing egg with it. The satisfaction of liberating the egg is still a gratifying result. Now I can enjoy my egg and my liberated words.

Here is a better metaphor for you to contemplate as you sit to write your poem: Boil the water, insert the tea bag and brew the contents. Take that tea bag, place it on a spoon, wrap the string tightly around the spoon and bag, squeeze the daylights out of it. If you can then get the leaves out of that bag, if you can read the leaves or find words in that mush, then you are not only becoming a better poet, but a better reader as well.

I leave you with this: Ezra Pound said that a good poem contains "absolutely no word that does not contribute to the presentation." Like any good document, the poem has to pass a due diligence test.

How will you next define your writing?

Poetic Diction

The definition of poetic diction is language employed in a manner that sets poetry apart from other speech or writing. In previous columns I talked about the creative use of language to achieve strong visual and sensual impacts in writing poetry. In this column, I hope to present a more philosophical, as opposed to mechanical, view of poetic language.

One of the most valid and valued occupations of poetry (and yes, poetry has an occupation) is the magical use of language. Why did I say "magical" instead of "practical"? The practical application of something could imply that this application or task has been practiced over and over again. Writing of poetry can and should do this (practice) of language continually. As writers we owe it to ourselves, and our readers, to always explore.

However, what I suggest here is the "magic" of language in poetry is it's transformative power. We read a piece and with that experience we are changed or transformed in some way. Thus, poetic diction. The poet, Mary Karr, in a recent issue of *Poetry Magazine,* wrote a compelling and disturbing poem, "The Burning Girl." She starts out the poem with these lines:

> "While the tennis ball went back and forth in time
> A girl was burning. While the tonic took its greasy
> Acid lime, a girl was burning..."

The poem goes on to draw us into a tennis match of comfort while describing the horrors of war. While we celebrated our independence somewhere, someone else suffered. Ms. Karr incorporated powerful language to make me uncomfortable and using the technique of "witness" I saw exactly what she described; and transformed my insinuation into the pain and suffering of a young girl.

Careful selection of words, which come together as language thus poetic diction, is what all poets strive to achieve. It is not enough, for me, to think in the everyday vernacular of my "internal dictionary." I keep several dictionaries on my desk to help me look for magical and transformative words. If I am going to tell a compelling story or draw in my readers so they are changed in some way, then I have to pull out all the creative stops I can.

Look at these lines from Edward Hirsch that he wrote in his elegy for his son, Gabriel:

> "I did not know the work of mourning / Is like carrying a bag of cement / Up a mountain at night…"

We feel that weight we cannot see, and in some way we are transformed.

How do you choose your magical language? How will your readers describe your poetic diction?

Concreteness & Abstraction in Our Poetic Language

As long as we have been writing and reading, and perhaps as we continued our writing education by taking extra courses or attending that prized workshop, we've certainly heard the old adage, "Show, don't tell." We are so fortunate that with all the words we have at our disposal, we can come up with ways to convey a particular image without having to state it. For example, instead of saying, "she was very sad," the practiced poet might say, "rivers of tears cascaded down her reddened face." The idea is to find strong, visual-inducing words to make the verse timeless and compelling.

Imagine you are a sculptor, working with clay that ultimately may be the model for a bronze piece. As the sculptor gathers the clay in his hands, feeling the texture, smoothing out the lumps, and begins to form his shape, your words should do the same thing. You select words from perhaps a journal; you examine them, feel them, say them out loud (how do they sound?). Now you begin your mental composition of the poetic piece, placing words here or there for emphasis and watching the poem take shape.

Your words can be concrete, meaning they refer to solid things, things we can touch or experience physically. Michael Palmer's lines:

> "The hills like burnt pages / Where does this door lead / Like burnt pages / Then we fall into something still called the sea…//"

are an example of concreteness. And, with a powerful simile included, too! Some other examples of concrete words: " cotton, grass, gallop, pony, raincoat."

What about abstraction, then? What if you want to be more general, perhaps a little vague or obscure, to create for your reader a path to ideas or insights? Abstract words provide us with ways to describe thoughts or things that cannot be touched. Examples of abstract words: *love, hope, peace, sadness*. Many poets write more in the abstract rather than the concrete, and sometimes we get lost in what they are saying to us. Some of the modern poets, such as John Ashbery and William Carlos Williams want poetry to be more specific, more concrete. Robert Penn Warren, in his poem *Unless* gives us great insight into when to be concrete and when to be abstract. Look at these lines:

> "All will be in vain unless?unless what? Unless / You realize that what you think is Truth is only / A husk for something else. Which might, / Shall we say, be called energy, as good a word as any, As when / The rattlesnake, among desert rocks / And Freudian cactus tall in moonlight, / Scrapes off the old integument, and floats away,... //"

When you write, will you feel how palpable your words are?

Interpretation

Previously, we've looked at a number of basic components. Here I want to take you on a side trip. This digression is meant to take you into the poetry cosmos of interpretation.

All the basics we have studied and used so far will not bring us any satisfaction until they coalesce into an accessible poem. Coleridge, so creative a poet, back in the late 18th or early 19th century, created the word, *esemplastic*, "to shape into one." Your readers will consider all possibilities when they read your words, listen as sounds form visuals, and ultimately form their own meaningful shape.

An excellent example of a poem that lends itself to wide interpretation, and likely even wider connection, is James Wright's, "Lying in a Hammock,...." The trigger finger of its last line, "I have wasted my life," exemplifies how surprise can arouse and connect. Another example is Elizabeth Bishop's, "The Fish." Her crisp, tight narrative, takes us right to the heart of fishing, and then propels us into a vast statement on the meaning of life. Read the complete poems, please!

Poets do wonderful things with their imaginations and words: They take us on a "magic carpet ride." When we write we can create this imaginative trip where we can let words run through our hair and lines tickle our eyes. And we can take this and ponder forever how a particular poem affected us.

When we compose our poetry, we can be active or passive. We can toss out clues or we can be opaque. Do we want our readers to see clearly or do we want them to "put on their mind's glasses" to bring it into focus? We can use repetitive sounds, hidden in words, to create visuals so subtle the reader almost misses them. But the thrill of reading these verses a second or third time, gives room for interpretation so the reader can have an "Aha!" moment-the big response.

Use your ordinary or everyday experiences to transform, to give you and your readers the poetic electrical charge which increases each time they return to your poems. Your writing can inspire the obvious disguised as the obscure, which can spring out like a wound-tight jack-in-the-box, leaving wonder for the reader. Poetry's ability to garner amazement is a key part of the magic. Think of these as the voltage meters: Who, What, Why, How, and When.

Until next time....

What I Mean Is...

When we've written our poem, say the first or at least an early draft, at this point we probably are thinking, "what did I just say?" To ponder over the words and initiate the process of extracting a meaning is our start on giving the reader a path to interpretation. We want our readers to take our poem(s), read them over and over again hopefully because they really like the renderings and can't get enough of them; but we also hope they find new meaning every time they read our writings. What we hope doesn't happen is that they keep reading because they are having difficulty figuring out what we said. For me, it is not satisfying for a reader to look up from the words and say, "this poem simply doesn't make sense to me".

Let's assume that you and I are writing a short narrative poem. We are contemplating some disturbing world event and we are so moved by this we want to write about it. How are we going to put this into words and give not only seriousness to it, but also maybe some insight or even hope for better things to come? Our poem will be a window for our readers. We contemplate what we see through that window pane, the clear class providing the illumination and clarity while in its closed state gives us some distance, some separateness. We see an act of violence perhaps and we want to make sense of why it happened; we want to tell about it in a way that draws out readers to either take some type of sympathetic action, or at least have their social consciousness raised.

Among the many notable writers and poets of war are Tim O'Brien and Bill Glose. Both used these settings to open our eyes about the events' effects on them and their comrades. Glose has written remarkable poetry about his Gulf War experience. In his poem, "Combat Art," his window is a canvas:

> "My canvas is a brown landscape / begging for splashes of color. / My brush is an M-16…"

Those are certainly not vague words. We can figure out what is likely coming next. So, his canvas poem is now our window to what he saw and experienced. In my poem, "General Jackson's Arm," I expose the reader to the horror of Stonewall Jackson losing his arm; but, what I am really talking about is my strong feelings about why the Civil War was fought. My window for the reader are these lines:

> "When Jackson lay there on this cot, maps and letters on his bed stand, / was there a clarifying and sudden wisdom, that comes from / having a limb sawed off?"

When we say what we mean, we hope the reader will get the meaning.

Relationships Within Poetry

In another column, I brought up the subject of "interpretation." We were encouraged in our writing to explore the use of words to give our poems broad meanings to our readers. Perhaps a poem would have a different meaning every time it was read by a single reader. This creates an interesting contradiction for both the poet and reader.

We have the poet setting up the subject matter of her poem. We have next the subject matter's relationship to the reader. We don't know how the poet's poem will be received, but the second the reader begins the poem, both have formed a relationship with the other. Now, as a writer and a poet, how do you form a relationship with your reader(s)? Do you write about your anger over particular current events? Do you engage your reader into protecting the environment? Do you write about a particularly lovely sunset?

Create your own syntax (how many times have I mentioned this word?). Let it provide your reader with your emotional relationship to the reader. You set the trap with your writing!

It all goes back to word choice, doesn't it? We affect so much of the reading community by our choice of words. The poet's magic is to put those words into meaningful lines, placed "expertly" in stanzas, and having those stanzas pull or push the reader into the poem. Because once the reader is in the poem, he or she is complicit in the work.

There are many ways to bring about the poem's contribution to creating a relationship. Writing about a moral dilemma, for instance, is a way to engage a reader with our poetry. Adding an element of the comic is another. Purposefully being ambiguous can set up a manipulation of the reader, which may make the reader uncomfortable, but also may make him think. We can write about our memories and see if we provide a common connection. The interpretation of a recurring dream lends itself to relationships. And we can further strengthen the relationship dynamic in the poem by using "we," instead of "I." In a "we" poem we simply provide the access and the reader now believes he has a relationship with us. We both ask and answer the questions provided by the poem.

One of the poets I admire and have mentioned before is Billy Collins. He hooks his readers into relationships by the expert use of humor as well as syntax. He is the master of engagement. How humorous it is to read his poem, "Pornography," Before even knowing what the poem is about, you are complicit with him. You want to know what the poem says. I won't spoil it for you here. I leave you to find the poem, learn from it, and then create your own relationship poetry.

Honorable Intentions

Think of this column as a continuation of a previous column, "What I Mean." One question I often ask myself when I'm composing is, do I really know what I am doing? Doesn't that sound comical? Of course, I know what I am doing. I'm writing, and if I work really hard at it, I am writing poetry. I'm not being ludicrous here. I submit that often as poets when we create something, we may not even be aware of the things we have created. A good example is reading Milton's *Paradise Lost*. Read in one context, it is a treatise on Christian doctrine. Read in another, it is classical poetry. In a segment on the description of Satan, we encounter such poetic words and lines. Consider:

> "...but his face / deep scars of thunder and intrenched, and care / Sat on his faded cheek, but under brows / Of dauntless courage, and considerate pride / Waiting revenge..."

In the context then of Milton and even more relevant of our times, when our readers take on our poetry, do they "own" the work? Of course, I don't mean anything to do with ownership, that is different. I mean their emotional investment. After all when we have someone read our finished piece, in a way, we have relinquished control, haven't we?

Recently a spoken-word artist/musician friend read my poem, "Stones for Words," at her music event. I had the joy of hearing her interpretation of my work, giving it her style as she read aloud my words. I was captivated by hearing another voice give life to my words from paper. I realized my intention of the poem: To impress upon someone other than myself that there was a message in that poem. She got it and in looking around the room I could see that others got it, too. That is how poetry works for me.

The last thing I want, as a poet, is to create a tug-of-war with my readers. If I start a conflict with a reader about my intention(s), in absence of face-to-face discussion, then I risk losing that reader (maybe forever!). Ideally, we as poets want our intentions and those of the readers to come together. This doesn't necessarily mean that the reader has to agree with us, but it does mean that our intention to give meaning should to be understood. We use our poetry to convey our thoughts, our dreams, our disappointments, our hopes, fears, and I could go on. We want all this exposure to connect with humanity and if our intention is to provide messages that will resonate, then we are creating honorable poetry. That's what Milton did, and that is what we can do.

Mimesis—Act of Expression

In 2016, I introduced columns with new ideas on the matters of poetry. I devoted my writing to more esoteric topics in hopes of drawing out the best in us when we wrote poetry. In previous columns we covered mechanics; and I have returned to them in different ways. But in this column, I speak to our inner motivations of writing poetry.

For one thing, it is not sufficient (in my opinion) to say, "I am a poet." I am not complete unless I say "I am a poet, and I have something to say." This is important. If we don't have something important to say, then nobody will care. Poetry compels us to have a passionate commitment to something. Our task is to find this something and write about it, poetically.

So, here goes with this column. The word, *Mimesis,* means to imitate. As a philosophical term it brings a lot of meanings, one of which is act of expression. I could further state that mimesis means a representation of reality, such as how Homer's *Odyssey* or Dante's *Divine Comedy* compares the world to how it appears in the *Bible.* All three are examples of long poems. All took very long times to compose and may have included contributions from more than one writer/poet.

Poets use the selection of words and presentation of lines and stanzas to present some type of testimonial. Poets want to be considered serious, don't they? Do poets want readers to believe that poets have taken time to be great writers? I believe they do. If poets couch their poems as testimonials of some observation (of nature, of relationships, world events etc.), they're not producing propaganda or party pamphlets, they're merely wanting to go on record that they are communicating via a literary genre.

The poet creates this piece, his or her place, outside the topic. Yet to succeed the reader must feel like he or she has been drawn inside it, like wandering through a fun house maze of mirrors. One reflects the poet; turn right or left, one reflects the reader. We can see the writings as distortions or we can see them as truths.

As you compose your thoughts and review your notes all in preparation for your new composition, think very hard about what you are about to say. You may be tempted to write everything down, do all the telling as it were. But bear this is mind: compression is a key technique. Think about what the poem is not. Think about white space that the reader imaginatively can fill in. Your message, your something to say, can convey extraordinary power by what it is not.

What's that you say?

My Poem as a Classic, or How Memorable Can I Be?

Think for a moment. What is a classic poem? I'm not referring to "The Classics," such as the poems of Homer, Virgil and Shakespeare. I'm talking now. How do we define, in today's poetry, what is a classic poem? Has the definition changed? What tests can be applied in today's poetry writing that determines whether or not it is, or perhaps will be a classic? Are we writing compelling enough poetry that our own humble offerings can stand any test that determines a potential classic?

I am bringing this up because as writers we know, on some level, likely very personal, that we want our writing to have an ongoing life away from us. We want our readership to grow and outlast us. We want readers to recall our words and with that recollection attribute this to some strong feeling they had about our poetry. Something like, "you know when Sara Robinson said, in her poem blah-blah, she really hit the nail hard. That was a classic view of the issue, in my opinion." Don't we all hope that we are giving something to readership and literature when that happens?

So, poetic writing as classic, in these modern times. What does it have to do, to go beyond being noticed? For starters, our language (and you read about this before from me) has to be strong and beautiful. It has to come together in remarkable ways that will ensure that the final piece will endure. When we write we have to think that our audience could be wider than we initially conceived. Our poetry has to become more universal, grander in scope. We take a bold risk that our writing could participate in social discourse or activism. Think Allen Ginsburg. Our home-grown literary giant, Mark Twain, said, "A classic—something that everybody wants to have read and nobody wants to read." That describes accurately my feeling about reading Dante's *Inferno*.

But if our poetry is pliable, then it accommodates the changes we encounter today. While T.S. Eliot felt that to be classic, everything [i.e. language, a person's mind] had to be mature, I've seen some profound wisdom come from young poets whose writing is definitely on a classical path. Our writing, to be classic, at least needs to be understood and appreciated differently by every generation. What if our writing can transcend timeliness? What if our words are so good that they will be appreciated and quoted for generations? Our verbiage is different from the 18th and 19th century masters, but that doesn't mean it won't last, in a classic way. I think Lesley Wheeler gives it to us, from her poem, *"The Sun Went Down When I Felt Sad, …"* "You're the only fisher who lives in my stanza. I would starve / without you…"

In the next two columns, I'll continue this theme by discussing epic, lyric poetry, and Barbara Kingsolver. Also check out Stephen Cushman's, *The Red List*. Written in a thoroughly modern presentation, he gives us endangered species, like the Bald Eagle in his the epic poem. "Some days it comforts to think of extinction…"

Epic Proportions

It only stands to reason that coupled with being a classic that the word, "epic," comes into play. Today we use this word far more expansively than its original definition. For example, our weather forecasters when naming storms describe them as having epic proportions; or that the devastation from the hurricane was an epic disaster. A cat lost from her family takes an epic journey across country to find them. You get the idea.

What does this have to do with my writing poetry, you ask? Well, I think that most of us who write, particularly poets, want to believe that inside of us lives a long, narrative poem about our lives, experiences, or even our dreams. This belief is similar to what we hear: Inside many writers resides a novel yet to be born. In our future epic, we, as heroes, could take a journey (one of the two types of master plots). We find ourselves conquering evil or doing something of nationalistic pride.

OK, then. Let's say we are going to write an epic poem. In today's arena, what does that mean? How long is the poem? Is there such a term as "modern epic"? Because we have widened the definition of "hero" beyond its original scope, how can we offer up an epic poem without making people uncomfortable? How do we give them a story of "epic proportions and significance" without trivializing the world? If we hope to bring our current and future readership into the fold, how can we best achieve this? And, recall I am talking now about introducing them to our poetic epic journey. Maybe our readers have not seen a long poem from us before. They may not have any expectations, real or otherwise. Our epic narrative may be one poem in a book of some 70-85 pages; or, it may be an epic tale which is broken up into individual poems presented as chapters. An example of this is Rita Dove, who won the Pulitzer Prize in 1987 for her long, narrative poem, *Thomas and Beulah*. And I'll further complicate this discussion by suggesting that the individual poems/chapters may be considered lyric poetry. More on this coming up.

Writing for readers now, our epic attempts must be an evolved narrative. I mean the narrative must reflect what is going on today, using today's language, and current ideas. The modern age, while it may not like long works of poetry, I have to believe would read something if it were that compelling. There are novelists whose poetic craft in their fiction writing provide them with the right "tools" to create compelling poetry. These are Margaret Atwood, Ron Rash, and Barbara Kingsolver. In her book, *How to Fly (In Ten Thousand Easy Lessons)*, Kingsolver provides epic poetry insight by hooking us first on titles, such as "How to Cure Sweet Potatoes." It closes with one of the best lines I've seen: "Recall this surrender when you sit down to eat them. / Consider the direction of your grace." Wow.

Lyric Outlasts Everything

First of all, let me start out by saying that the fourth edition of *The Princeton Encyclopedia of Poetry and Poetics* (2012, Princeton University Press) devoted nine pages to the history, definition, and modern description of lyric poetry. All you ever wanted to know is there. What I want to do with this column is discuss how we as poetry writers can interpret today's lyric style and apply it to our writing.

First of all, likely when you think of lyric, you think of words set to music. That's logical since lyric is derived from "lyre." However, as good as song lyrics are, some circles would not consider them poetry. Try telling that to Bob Dylan! Some would argue that musical lyrics are not poetry because the music comes first, then the words are set to fit the music. I'm not sure I agree, but then I want to think that much of the poetry I write, okay maybe a little of what I write, is so good that it could be set to music. If that should happen, would my poem cease to exist then?

Teachers of poetry often used poems of Robert Browning to illustrate what lyric poetry is. One of the reasons why is that these poems, for the most part, have a single speaker who is waxing philosophically (or romantically) on some topic. His poetic style has often been described as "dramatic monologue." A famous example is his classic poem, "My Last Duchess." There are some other attributes assigned to lyric poetry that we should note: brevity, passion, compression, and subjectivity. As the poem progresses it should unfold in such as way that there seems to be an inherent musicality or harmony to it.

W.B.Yeats was considered by many critics as "the most gifted lyricist of his century." He wrote into the 20th century so I consider him transitional to the modern poet. My favorite lines are from his poem, *"Sailing to Byzantium."* "That is no country for old men. The young / In one another's arms, birds in the trees / —Those dying generations— at their song, …"

When we set out to describe our poetry as lyrical then we must think of the amount of passion we put into words and lines. Think of how you (as possible hero/heroine) are travelling through the context of your poem. Do you have heroic struggle and then success? Can you write pointedly and sensuously about this? How large is your vocabulary to fit your emotional commitment to the verse? One of the techniques I use to compose my lyric attempts is to look at the words and lines of musical artists I admire to see if I can find unusual or extraordinary words or rhyme schemes. Bob Dylan is a favorite source and so are Paul Simon and Aimee Mann.

Good hunting!

The Gist of the Subject

We've discussed quite a bit on the mechanics of poetry. And we've discussed interpretation and relationships within poems. But now I interrupt the program to discuss the "subject" of a poem. Stephen Dobyns, in his book, *Next Work, Better Word*, the craft of writing poetry, referenced George Saintsbury's four great requirements of poetry: "say something; say it with strict limits of form and very strict space limits; say it forcibly; and, say it beautifully."

This is all well and good, but how do we select subject matter to which we apply the four requirements? When we set about our mission of creating poems, our poetry, there likely is some type of idea or level of importance as to what we want to say. We could say that the subject matter is our destination and the words we select (our poetic language) and all the other tools are our luggage, tickets, and transport to get us there.

Our primary goal is that our selected topics will enhance the human experience. We can cover the depths of emotions to the boundless beauty of nature to our dismay at certain world events. But, unlike prose writers, (unless we are delving into prose poetry), we must be succinct. Our words may have to be metaphorical (as we read about previously). We will rely on our readers to take the journey with us in amazing ways.

Recently I discovered the poetry of Arthur Rimbaud (1854-1891). Between the ages of 17 and 20, he contributed more to poetry than many do in lifetimes. He was quite influential on modern verse (and he didn't even know how much!). He used his skill of language to take the subject of love to a remarkable level, as noted in his poem, "Romance." Modern poets, such as Elizabeth Bishop and Adrienne Rich, have written about love in such ways that these poems will never age. That to me is how a poem's subject can go beyond being relevant.

All of this seems like more of form and content, and true it is. But what I hope to differentiate here is that in order for form and content to work their planned magic, we have to have something to say. We don't have to pick something so profound that we can't even write about it. Often, a successful poem on the topic of death will focus on the death of a beloved pet. We can sense all the encompassing grief; and feel the immediacy of such strong emotion. The strength of that sadness can expand to how we react to death as a global human experience. The emotion is the emotion. This is how poetry connects us.

The Turn

As part of discussion on "closure" of a poem, I will discuss "the turn." For some critics and writers, this may be considered the heart of a poem's purpose. Often described as the point where either a surprise is created or a previously presented argument is now answered. The turn indicates a shift.

Historically, sonnets have often been the most frequent place to observe the turn. One can observe it in Shakespeare, or even more in contemporary poems by Marianne Moore, Edna St. Vincent Millay and Elizabeth Bishop. For example, in the sonnet, usually the first seven or so lines present an argument or position, if you will. Then the remaining six or so lines give the response or solution or counter point. Look at Millay's "Sonnet xxx" to see how she worked the turn.

Sometimes a beginning word of the pivotal line leads one right into the turn. Examples of leading words are: *then, though, but, or, however, so, unless,* etc. In contemporary poetry, such as that written by Moore or William Carlos Williams, the enjambment presents the turn as line breaks create the turn. There is a certain tension or even energy that moves us along using line breaks to guide us around a corner, as it were. Moore's poem, "That Harp You Play So Well," exemplifies this.

Stanza breaks, end words wrapping around lines, even prepositions, all carefully considered can be our creative tools to write remarkable poems with remarkable closures. As the poem leads us we can create lines that provide a narrative direction, hinting of the metaphor, presenting information, giving more depth and meaning.

So, we want the turn to create something else the reader needs to think about. It can be a change in tense which creates a kind of deception, or it can be a clarification of a different meaning or point. In all cases the turn should be a reversal. Why? Maybe we want the reader to go back to the beginning of our poem, and given the opportunity to fully understand what is going on in the poem. Sometimes I think there is a kind of oddness to poetry, that a turn can show. As if in its oddness the turn can explain everything.

How do I get to a meaningful turn in my own poetry? I look as far inside the poem as I possibly can. Does each word require dissection? Maybe. Some words may require rejection, too. All must work to achieve what I want the reader to know.

We want our poetry to create a probability of interruption so that this pause in the poem's flow can make the poem powerful. A poem like "Traffic" by Tomas Tranströmer offers us a practical consideration.

Moving Closer To the Close

In a previous column, I talked about "the turn," and its role as a poem heads toward its inevitable close. One of the joys in writing a poem is reaching a satisfying conclusion or some type of end that brings all the aspects of the poem together. Sometimes the conclusion can be fulfilling; sometimes it's philosophical; sometimes it leaves the work open for further discussion; and sometimes the end is simply a surprise. Academics who study particular poets have written volumes or at least a lot of essays in attempts to interpret and analyze what the particular poet was saying. And often these studies are driven by how particular poems concluded.

Do you want to be like how Rita Dove wrote about Billie Holiday? "If you can't be free, be a mystery." Sometimes I really work at making my poems sufficiently obscure that I hope to tease a reader into re-reading and re-reading. One of the techniques I employ is an ending line or two, which offers a "twist" to the previous content of the poem. It's comparable to leaving a possible argument or contradiction. And while this relates in that aspect to the "turn," I differ in that I put this at what I consider the end or close of the poem.

What all this boils down to is: How do you want your poem to "go out"? How does this particular poem compare to others you have written or to others you have read? Think about poems that particularly affected you, and your writing. I have several favorite poets whose choice of words not only inspires me, but also how these words work to come to close, and really give me the intellectual boost I need to keep improving.

One of the poets I admire is James Wright (1927-1980). His poem, "Lying in a Hammock at William Duffy's Farm in Pine Island, Minnesota," is frequently anthologized. One reason why is the last line, "I have wasted my life." Why do I like that? This poem concludes after we "see" him reclining and watching all the marvels of nature either fly over or blow by. He hears sounds of cowbells; he sees droppings from horses of last year. He realizes how much he may have missed in his life because he didn't observe closely all the wonderful things around him. And, this is especially important in that the poem reveals all this to the reader, simply, without detailed or exhausting analysis, in five short words.

As we approach the end of our newly-created poem, we can hope that reader exploration can take many paths: some complex, some simple. Maybe our poem raises questions. But with a powerful close, at the very least, our poem will give a remarkable experience. Take a look at your last couple of lines. Surprise?

Revision or I Have a "Write" to Change My Mind.

This is the first of two columns on this topic. The other morning when I wrote a poem, I thought I was almost finished. I gave it a few tweaks before lunch, and a couple more before dinner. Then both poem and I rested overnight. So, the next morning I looked at my masterpiece first thing and my immediate thought was: *what was I thinking? Or writing?* There was not a word or line here I liked. I wondered if someone stole into my house and sabotaged my papers! Haven't we all been there? What were originally thought to be good lines didn't even make any sense.

This happens for me probably more frequently than I would like to admit. One of the toughest things I've had to learn as a writer, especially of poetry, is to forgive myself for writing badly. I now have a sign over my desk: *Get It Down, Then Get It Good.* One huge epiphany for me has been that while the craft of poetry emerges from experience; the endurance arrives from revision. Once we get "out of our heads" and onto the paper we can utilize the analytical parts to pull the narrative together. Judgment balances freedom, control soothes flight; and tidiness keeps us from scatter. We learn how we know when to do this and how much is part of how we explore, define, and grow our writing, by revision. An irony of writing is being subjective about our own writing. That is a huge conflict, it would seem, but think about how validated you would feel if you could stand back and seek approval from yourself for your writing. Revision is a way to do this. There may be much unseen or even untapped energy still in that poem that has not fully emerged. Revision can be a source of liberation. Think of this like stirring a pot of pasta sauce where you have added different seasonings throughout the simmer. With each stir a new aroma comes forth that, left unstirred, might not have hit the air. Now you can tantalize your readers.

In the meantime, relating to revision, when we revise, we must make sure we don't force an ending simply because it sounds good. We have to make sure we resolve the poem. The poem will not bring any satisfaction if it is left "hanging."

Want to try a revision "trick"? Take a poem, rewrite it using the last line as the first line and see what happens.

More on revision next time…

Revision, Part II. Write, Re-Write, Right

Now that we are fully engaged with the thought of revision, I want to discuss the intangible elements of revision. What are these? Well, I'm thinking of emotions, aesthetic influences, self-understanding, self-knowledge, and risk taking. Why are these important?

For starters, I look at these as paths to liberation. I set myself free and embrace the revision. I've got the essence of the poem I want to write down. I have the essence of what I want to say. I'm comfortable that my metaphor works. Now I have to take off the restraints and give my revision a vote, perhaps the voice.

This is the part of writing poetry I enjoy. To me, it is like I'm translating my poetry into my poetry. I approach this not unlike how Ezra Pound approached translating Chinese poetry. He, without any knowledge of Chinese, would take a translator's rendition and convert it into the imagist style he created. He used a "technique" called *compression*. In other words, use no more words than you have to. If the words don't contribute to the image or the message or the theme, then take them out. I like the word, "distillation." I like to think that I've got a product in the making. I am going to distill the contents, looking for the best components to rise to the top, then I am going to age it for a bit, and see what emerges. If it suits, then, my tastes, I likely will conclude it is finished.

I don't know how great poets look at revision. When we read their poems, likely we are not reading the first, or even the tenth, version of the poem. We probably won't ever know unless we are able to talk to the living ones. But looking at the poetry of Ellen Bass, one of my muses, I have to admire how her poems come together and I have to think that when she wrote her poems, she let them simmer for a while. The poems are so good, so complete, so powerful. Take her poem, "Relax," from her latest book, *Like a Beggar*. She opens the poem with "Bad things are going to happen." What a great opening line! The poem is thirty-seven lines long and by the time the poem is finished with the last line, "crunch between your teeth," a lot has happened.

Among our challenges in finishing our poems is the ending. We want to conclude our poems with a sense of finality, right? We've accomplished our primary goal of stating something in our poem, whether it is short or long. Our syllables have formed to create a poetic density. We aren't satisfied until this "texture," this compression of words, syllables, and lines has fulfilled its mission: A poem of clarity and beauty which ends leaving the reader wanting more.

Leave your readers begging for more!

Crossing the Finish Line

In a previous column, "Moving Closer to the Close," I talked about how you may choose to end your poems. What words would lead to a satisfactory conclusion. In this column, I'm talking about the same idea, only different. How do you know when the poem or poetic work (i.e. book-length or multipage poem) is finished? It is not enough, for me, to exclaim, "I'm done." I have to complete the project (as it were). Like a carpenter who measures twice, cuts once, I have to revise and think, think and revise. Have I said all I wanted to say in this poem? How do I know when I have concluded with the draft and now have the final piece? Maybe we never totally finish a poem. We can't ask Elizabeth Bishop why she kept on revising. We can't ask Gwendolyn Brooks why she kept all her notes and clippings. I have at least 3 spiral notebooks going all the time (including where this piece started!) in which I tape articles, cartoons, poems, all sorts of flotsam and jetsam I come across. These come in handy as writing tools, prompts, and path markers to create a poem.

Often I finish a poem like an essayist completes a treatise, when I have put in the only possible conclusion I can reach at that moment—for that poem. I give myself a reason for why this particular poem exists, put in my lines to state my feelings or observations, or thoughts, construct my form, select my words; then look where I need to put the "turn," and head for the finish.

I strive for the "a-ha" moment and if I can say it, there's a darn good chance this poem is finished. But, and this is a big one, just so you know, I have many, many unfinished poems. Lots of us poets have unfinished poetic symphonies. It's a very crowded field heading toward the finish line. I have great fun and feel much satisfaction when I can cross that line. Sometimes I don't want to actually cross it; I like the process so much.

At the end of the day, however, I like more the satisfaction of knowing that I have finished a piece. To see and appreciate the work process and reflect on how I got from start to finish is very satisfying for me. I also realize and appreciate that writing, at least for me, is not a team sport. Like horse racing, getting to the finish line is all about your own personal pace, and your approach. You don't have to look to see where anyone else is so you don't have to be distracted or pressured. You can look out your window in your writing space, and think, "I'll get there, and when I do, it will feel so good."

Finding the "Write" Title (s) For Your Poem (s)

After all this reading, writing, revising, more of what I just wrote—have you thought of a title for your poem (s)?

Titles are viewed by many writers as the hardest part of finalizing the poem. In fact, some poets never give a title to a work, using "Untitled" as the "title." Emily Dickinson's poems are numbered, for example. And she's not even the one who numbered them. All of her poems were published after her death.

What is the purpose of the title, or what does it do? For one, the title provides a clue as to the subject of the poem. Even then, an obscure title can be tricky to a reader. Philip Levine, in his poem, *"The Horse,"* leads us at first glance to think of a horse, but actually the poem is about the bombing of Hiroshima. Ah, the wonder of the metaphor. The writer might compose the title from a few key words in the poem. Sometimes, the title can have the expected effect or even the result of what is going on in the poem. You may find, as I often do, that your title gets revised as you are revising your poem.

However, if we simply use "Poem" as the title then we either force or trust the reader to be curious enough to read the poem. For me, that is a big chance to take. I want and need readers! If the title is the bait, then we need them to take it, lines and all, to what follow next.

Poetry is all about "getting it." The title is the first step. Here are a few titles (with poet) that I selected because they grabbed my attention: "Skunk Hour" (Robert Lowell); "The Shampoo" (Elizabeth Bishop); "Why I Am Not a Painter"

(Frank O'Hara); and "The Next-to-Last Canary Speaks" (Sara Robinson).

Just think of this: You've constructed this wonderful building that is your poem. And as in real life construction, where the crew tops it off with a tree, you top yours with a grand title.

How will you title your personal masterpiece?

AT LAST

The Defense of Poetry

Are we responsible for making poetry matter? How do we prove or defend the idea that poetry can make a difference? How will our lines influence society in general, our own lives, or even the conservation of nature? Do we use poetry to expose a morality of bad taste?

What about the use of hyperbole to create a defense of poetry? It could be noted that the use of extreme exaggeration, in a line, to make a point could risk overwhelming the entire poem. Or does the entire poem work as hyperbole?

How can we find a balance as part of our defense of poetry? Author Michael Robbins, in his new book, *Equipment for Living: On Poetry and Pop Music* (Simon & Schuster) stated, "No one has ever changed his life because of a poem or song…" Really? Why do I find that hard to accept?

On a personal note, a young woman heard me read my poem, "A Poem Written As Scars," came up to me and said my poem changed her life. Later in the same book, [Robbins] also says, "There is no limit to what a poem can't do…poetry makes all sorts of things happen." These statements add to the confusion of how best to defend poetry.

Poets, since the beginning of the genre itself, have used its form to confront grief, describe horrors of war, starvation, and suicide. We have learned about the complexities of human lives through poetry. Witness Sylvia Plath and Robert Lowell. The tragedies of mental illness, for example, are laid bare with these and others. Poetry provides insight and intimacy without which we might not understand how precious life is.

Poetry has emboldened people to reveal mental turmoil, has given us the heartland of America, and has enlightened us. Poetry may not give any one person everything or every answer. Humans are too individual for universal acceptance. But what would we have, if we didn't have poetry?

I often say at readings, "While poetry is mostly fiction, it always states great truths." For many poetry is more accessible than philosophy and in this access people gain their sense of worth, as to why they are even here. When we read poetry about the wonders of nature, the sentiments of love, and the sadness of death, we share the experience with the writer. We also gain the sense of hope. Perhaps that one sense is the most important gift of poetry. Hope.

Poetry can be experienced alone or in public. Tea-sippers and whisky enthusiasts can appreciate poetry. When we share poetry at gatherings connections are formed that add to the value of the human experience. Poetry can help us fall asleep or it can keep us awake and energized into action. We may not "binge-read" poetry, but I can show you books I could not put down until I finished. That's another defense: poetry books are typically less than 100 pages, easier to complete at a sitting and easier to pick up for repeat readings. It is easier to carry a poetry book in one's purse than a novel!

Even single lines can be poetry. How marvelous is that? Think about this line:

"I fix upon what would give me pleasure in my average moments..." (Marianne Moore)

When we read poetry in our average and spare moments we can gain pleasure. Who doesn't love Mary Oliver? Here is a three line stanza from her poem, "Landscape," that I believe is so powerful:

> "Every morning I walk like this around / the pond, thinking: if the doors of my heart / ever close, I am as good as dead."

What an incredible validation of how our own personal openness can enrich our lives.

Louis Menand, in a review titled, "The Defense of Poetry," for *The New Yorker* magazine, wrote, "When the going gets stressful, the stressed want poems."

Amen to that.

Turning the Poem Over to the Poem

What is this, you say? I'm sure our novelist friends would agree that when they are in the thicket of their manuscript, they find that the book actually writes itself and the author is simply the tool who gets it down on paper. Sometimes the main character or characters take over and all we can do is let her or them do their thing.

Actually this same thing can happen in poetry. Perhaps not so much in a short poem, but I can see it definitely happening in a long narrative poem. Three modern poets who I follow have, I believe, provided poetry done this way: Natasha Trethewey, Rita Dove, and Lesley Wheeler. In fact, Lesley, also a personal friend, wrote a masterful book, *The Receptionist,* in terza rima (a rhyming verse form used by Dante). The reading community received a treat with, *brown girl dreaming*, by Jacqueline Woodson. This marvelous example of brilliant narrative written as verse won the National Book Award. Using her childhood as inspiration, she let the poetry expand her story and draw us in.

So, how do we know when our poem is about to take us over? I'm not sure, but for me there is this kind of moment when I am writing that I realize I've put words down and was on some level not aware that I had done that. Maybe when we feel like our poetry is surprising us is when we know the poem has taken over. When I look back and re-read some pieces, and I ask myself, did I really write that, I have to believe the poems had taken over.

When deeply engaged with a poem, I sit back and let my mind wander. In this state I may not be writing anything, but I'm letting go of my immediate ownership. Sometimes this works, sometimes not. When this does work, I sense the poem I'm working on has taken stock of me and what I am trying to say. Again, I stay tuned in to ensure my word choices work.

At last we come to the fun part: The end or close. So, does the poem tell me when to stop or do I? In a previous column, I discussed the close and how one knew when or how to close the poem. The decision, at this point, for me is to take back the poem and decide how I want to end. The final contribution is bringing the poem to a natural and unforced conclusion. The close may require several edits or revisions to get it right, for you.

With that, I'll close for now…

To Workshop or Not To Workshop?
Is That a Question?

I have often fielded calls from writers about workshops and should they join one. Have I had any experience with a workshop? What did I learn? Would I attend another? Do famous poets/writers present workshops? What about critique groups? These are all very good questions, and very tough for me to answer. But I'll start with some basic responses.

Yes, I have had experience with workshops, both in attending and running. For the most part I benefitted from them. One basic thing to consider: A workshop is not necessarily a critique group. When I started my workshop many years ago, I had one purpose: To work with writers to get their works ready for publication. As such we were taking already composed pieces ready for ordering into a manuscript or for sending out to journals (and similar), and polishing them for completion.

A critique group, by contrast, is helping writers in the formative stages of their renderings by giving them basic feedback. While I have done both, I really don't have a preference except that for nine years I have been facilitating a poetry literary critique group where we read and discuss poets already known. Think Auden, Wordsworth, Rita Dove, John Keats, Mary Oliver, etc.

Let's get back to workshops, however. The first question you may ask yourself is what do you want to get out of being in a group with other writers? If you are already published and you want to sharpen your skills, a critique group may be useful. I've found critique groups helpful when I am concerned about audience reception to what I've written. As you can see, there can be a gray area between the two groups.

So, the second question you may ask relates to the group itself. What is their purpose and what are their goals? Look online for workshops. Explore magazines that deal directly with writing, such as *Poets & Writers* or *Writers Digest*. They have excellent resources in their monthly publications which can often be found at public libraries.

A next question is a tough one: How receptive are you to constructive criticism about your work? If you are very sensitive, workshopping may not be your thing. But if you can accept that everyone there is coming for the same reason, you may find the experience exhilarating. Often, and again depending upon the workshop set-up, there are writing prompts, shared experiences, tips on publishing, and loads of useful help.

I will promise you this: Whatever you may have thought about revision, discard it. Revision is the soul and heartbeat of good writing. Attending a workshop will show you how to embrace your inner "revisionist." Personally, I love revision. You would be surprised to know how many poems I have created from revised lines taken out of another text.

So, for you, think about a value you can gain from joining a workshop. Perhaps you can find one as part of a writers retreat close by. Think, too, of kindred spirits gathered on a blanket at the end of a perfect day reading and discussing each other's contributions, perhaps with a nice iced tea or white wine. What an amazing opportunity! Until next time…

Engagement with Poetry (or How to Propose to Your Friends)

There is a widely popular rock song in which the singer says to someone else, *"Put a ring on it."* Now how does this relate to us and poetry? Well, both suggest a proposal and a follow-up commitment. But how do we get friends and acquaintances to commit? To poetry?

Let's look at some of the ways our poetry can present the "ring."

Metaphor is a great starting place as that is one of the main tasks of a poem. I've written about this in earlier columns, but let's take a brief review. Metaphor, by definition, is where one thing is likened to another. From a poetic perspective, we could say an implied comparison where a word or phrase is taken out of its usual context and given a new meaning. A famous example is John Donne's "No man is an island."

In the beginning of this book, I started out by writing, "On a sunny, unremarkable day, I see poetry lying in an ordinary ditch." Similes are often used as another type of comparison. In using simile, we often use the words, "like," and "as." For instance, "my body is like an old battered bourbon barrel."

What about passion and intensity as rules of engagement? Can we be so devoted to poetry that we channel our enthusiasm into words convincing our audience that poetry is passion?

I love it when someone says, "I don't like poetry." When I ask why, she/he always responds about hating it in high school or even college, where studying poetry was part of the English requirement. I tell my friends to forget all that. I didn't prefer the old poets then either. But now, we have such marvelous writers that cover the entire spectrum of topics. Tired of listening to any politician or pontificant? Read an activist's poetry. Start with our current U.S. poet laureate, Joy Harjo. Rejoice in her amazing wordsmithing. Try to write like her!

Share your other favorite poets with your friends, then talk about the uniqueness of their writing. Other poetry can influence your own. You can study by imitating writing.

After the engagement party is over, what is next. Keep writing and keep looking for more inspiration. Here is a line from Morrigan McCarthy that sums up everything: *"...poetry allows for beauty in the messiness and mystery of being human."* I wish I had written that; but what I can tell you is that poetry will transform your friends. And if any one of them comes back to remark about one of your poems, and what it meant to them, then the engagement proposal was a success!

Practice proposing!

Am I Done With This Poem?

When is a poem finished? How do you know when you have reached the end of your poetry piece? For some of you who have kept up with either my Southern Writers columns or my Suite T blogs, this may sound like I am resurrecting old stuff. But hang in there with me, I have some new things to say about finishing a poem.

When we are writing, and we believe we are coming to the end of the poem, the "finish line," as it were, are we saying that the poem is good at this time? Is there more to write, or have I written too much? And now when I go back, I realize I finished the poem in several places before I came to my perceived "end." Was I really done? Is where I am really "good"?

How many poems have you read, where you asked if the poet really meant to stop there? I've read my share, and that includes my own. Some poets stop intentionally before they finish. Does that seem odd? Sure, we read a poem, think that the poet stopped too soon. But that is our opinion. We can't guess intention. Take this ending from Billy Collins' poem, "Hippos on Holiday": "Only a mean-spirited reviewer / would ask on holiday from what?" Of course, this ending is taking out of context, but he does end the poem with a question mark, which is a great way to leave the reader to determine for herself whether the poem is done.

Now you ask, where am I going with this? I want to convey that good poems need to come across as finished. When you say the poem is done, in your view, the poem is good when it is done.

I often choose many endings or closings for one poem. I have to have enough plans for when I decide I am done, and what I have written is good. This is when revision becomes important. I know. I know. Many poets hate to revise. But I've shared this before: I love revision. Between when I create the first rendering and when I finish the piece, I might go through five to ten or more versions. And when I finally settle on something, this is how the poem tells me it is done.

Here is a little trick I use: I reverse the order of the poem to see if the first line is a better ending than the last line. You might find yourself surprised if you try this.

I have finally gotten to the point: The poem will tell you when you are done. When you write, listen and read carefully so you don't miss hearing, " that's it, we're done. And it is good."

Are you finished?

How to Conduct a Reading of Your Poetry

Now you have read all the previous columns, you have amassed an impressive collection of poems, and you are ready to read them out loud. What? To the public, of course. You are ready to share, and you need to prepare for presentation. Let's pretend, then, you are gathering your "forces" to make your appearance.

Here are some things to consider not in any particular order:

*Choose your attire carefully. Consider monochromatic colors. These will not take the eyes away from you as a whole person. If your audience is wondering what shade of fuchsia you are wearing, they will miss your poems.

* Decide if you want to sit or stand. Personally it depends on the venue. However if you stand, your voice will project better.

* Make eye contact with your audience. This is hard, but it is so essential. Don't gaze upward into the heavens as you read. Your inspiration comes from the page.

* Give some backstory about yourself, but don't go into detail about the story behind each poem. Leave time for questions.

* Don't be afraid to read your poems. It is not necessary to memorize, then recite.

* Always open your event by reading a poem by another poet. This helps spread the inclusiveness of poetry. I like to start with Ellen Bass's, "Until You Return."

* Speak clearly and practice, beforehand, any pronunciation of difficult words.

* Take a variety of your poetry with you so you can select based on your interaction with the audience.

* Keep a bottle of water next to you.

* At the end of your reading, which you should keep under twenty minutes, don't forget to thank your audience for attending and supporting the literary arts.

Now that you are there to read, here are some other considerations:

* Have you published a book or chapbook? Take copies to sell or give away.

* Always have a pen, preferably one that does not bleed through paper.

* When signing, always ask and repeat back the spelling of the recipient's name.

Last: Did you have fun? If yes, then plan for another one. If no, ask why not? Then set about to turn this around.

I can't wait to hear you read...

When We Wrap Works Up & Move On

So, now we have closed in on the final essay in this collection. We've been through all the mechanics, ideas, parts and parcels of what we can use to write our poetry. How does it feel to know you are successfully engaging in your craft?

I want to leave you with one final thought: Writing poetry is a transactional relationship. I recently learned this term when I took a class on tying flies for fly fishing. The art/craft of tying flies is very similar to the art/craft of writing poetry. Both rely on convincing another party (fish or person) to "take the bait." With poetry, our metaphorical "hook" is generally the first line. If you are to concentrate on one particular component of your poetry, then really give that first line attention. Unlike fiction, where the writer has pages to engage the reader, we poets have a shorter line space to pull a reader in. Just like the perfect tie to catch a trout, we need the best line we have to complete the transaction.

Poets spent a "writing lifetime" constructing a poem which will either be read in minutes or dismissed in a moment. Back to the wary trout: I might spend forty-five minutes constructing an appealing nymph (to me anyway), only to have my intended catch ignore it. We sure don't want our intended audience to ignore us!

As you have seen throughout this book, there is no right or wrong way to write a poem. Yes, there are some basics that need attention and possibly correction to make the poem work. Those are your "tools." I use 3 x 5 notecards with my mechanics written on them. I carry them with me everywhere in my writer's satchel. Did you notice I did not use the word, "toolbox"? That has become a cliché and my advice is to never use that phrase, "tools in my toolbox."

While we are at the end of this edition, we are either beginning or continuing our poetry writing. I hope you will always write to your heart's content. I hope you will share your love of poetry with others. May the fire that is within your words, give warmth and happiness to your world, however large you want it to be.

Until next time…

SUGGESTED READING

Some of What's in My Library

Auden, W.H. *The Selected Poetry Of...* Modern Library Books. 1958

Bass, Ellen. *Like a Beggar.* Copper Canyon Press. 2014

Bishop, Elizabeth. *The Complete Poems, 1927-1979.* 1989

Brooks, Cleanth & Robert Penn Warren. *Understanding Poetry.* (4th Ed.). Harcourt Brace. 1976

Clampitt, Amy. *The Kingfisher.* Alfred A. Knopf Publishing. 1983

Collins, Billy. *The Rain in Portugal.* Random House. 2016

Dennis, Carl. *Poetry as Persuasion.* The University of Georgia Press. 2001.

Dickinson, Emily. *The Complete Works Of...* (Thomas Johnson, ed.) Back Bay Books. 1961

Dove, Rita. *On the Bus with Rosa Parks.* W.W. Norton. 1999

Laux, Dorianne. *What We Carry.* BOA Editions. 1994

Lerner, Ben. *The Hatred of Poetry.* Farrar, Straus, & Giroux. 2016

Longenbach, James. *The Virtues of Poetry.* Graywolf Press. 2013

Mayes, Frances. *The Discovery of Poetry.* (A Field Guide to Reading and Writing Poems). Harcourt, Inc. 2001

Wright, C.D. *The Poet, the Lion, Talking Pictures, El Farolito, a Wedding in St. Roch, the Big Box Store, the Warp in the Mirror, Spring, Midnights, Fire & All.* Copper Canyon Press. 2016.

SARA M. ROBINSON
1623 RIVERWALK XING
CHARLOTTESVILLE, VA 22911

SUMMARY: Over thirty years of sales, sales management, product development and executive marketing experience in the chemical and minerals processing industries. Proven abilities include new business development, distributor network establishment and management, new product development and new market introductions. Over ten years experience in creative writing, specifically poetry.

EXPERIENCE AND ACCOMPLISHMENTS
2009-Present: Sara Robinson Consultants and Sara Robinson, Author, Charlottesville, VA.
Sara Robinson Consultants is principally involved in the development and application of minerals, specifically wollastonite, mica, talc, feldspars, and silicas in selected niche industries.

Sara Robinson, published author, focuses on creative writing, particularly poetry, memoir, and short story genres. She has founded a workshop and instructed poetry composition and critique within the UVA system.
Has won several poetry awards and been published in a variety of journals and anthologies. Note: Her professional writing resume is a separate document.

2000-2009: Retired with R.T. Vanderbilt Co., Inc. Norwalk, CT - Business Development Manager-Minerals for a 500+ employee company involved in chemical manufacturing, minerals mining and processing and chemical distribution of products for the rubber, plastics, petroleum, ceramics, paints, personal care, and construction products industries.
*Primary responsibility is development and marketing of wollastonite to the engineered thermoplastic polymer markets and the paint and coatings sector.
*Developed and successfully introduced 10 new grades of wollastonite.
*Secondary responsibility is development of new markets and expansion of current markets for the company's bentonite and magnesium aluminum silicate products.
*Team leader for the group which successfully launched new bentonite grade for the natural personal care market.

1998-2000: Fibertec, Inc. Bridgewater, MA.
Director of Business Development for 60 employee company involved in the processing and marketing of mineral and milled glass products for

the plastics, coatings, friction and construction products industries.
*Responsible for the technical and market application developments for wollastonite, mica, mineral wool and other niche mineral products.
*Developed and successfully commercialized new grade of wollastonite for use as chopped glass replacement in thermoset resin polymer composites.
*Successfully commercialized new grade of wollastonite for use in powder coatings.
*Successfully commercialized new grade of processed mineral wool fiber for the automotive friction market.

1993-1998: NYCO Minerals, Inc. Willsboro, NY (formerly a division of Fording Coal and Canadian Pacific, now is owned by the Imerys Corporation.

NYCO is 120 employee company involved in the mining, processing, and marketing of a specialized mineral for the construction, plastics, friction, ceramics, coatings, and metallurgical industries.

General Manager, Marketing-Ceramics, Coatings, Distributors (1997-1998). Position was assigned after decentralizing USA operations and merging with parent company (Fording Coal).
*Developed successful and resultant patent for new end-use application for wollastonite in ceramics.
*Successfully initiated the first large volume sales of wollastonite products from the new Mexican facility to both ceramic and coatings sectors.

Director of Sales & Marketing (1993-1997)
*Responsible for direction and execution of company's annual sales budgets. Since 1994 (first year of personal responsibility) has successfully guided a 15% increase over budget in tons sold and sales revenue.
*Implemented and directed establishment of product marketing strategy segments resulting in sales expansion into Latin America and Asia.
*Team participant in the presentation of business growth justifying decision to purchase reserves which led to construction of processing plant in Mexico.
*Responsible for the management, budge achievement, and training of North American distributor network. Since 1994 **budget** achievement (as measured by >100% of budget) was accomplished by 80% of distributors.

1991-1993: Heucotech, Ltd. Fairless Hills, PA

Regional Sales Manager for 60+ employee manufacturer of pigments and dispersions for the graphic arts, coatings, and plastics industries.
*Directed development and expansion into the textile industry resulting in new sales of over $1million in first year of expansion.
*Guided the company's decision to apply for a patent and to develop market for unique titanium dioxide-based high-performance pigment.

1984-1991: Hitox Corporation of America (now owned by United Minerals Company). **Corpus Christi, TX**
60+ employee processor and marketer of inorganic pigments and functional fillers for coatings, plastics, and construction products industries.
   Vice-President, Sales & Marketing (1986-1991)
   National Sales Manager (1984-1986)
*Developed and directed sales from $3.7 million in 1985 to over $15 million in 1990.
*Guided the introduction of BARTEX® barium sulfate fillers in 1985 to sales of over $3 million in 1990.
*Guided the introduction of HALTEX® aluminum trihydrate products in 1985 to sales of over $3 million in 1990.
*Guided the introduction of OSO® iron oxide pigments in 1987 to sales of over $2 million in 1988.
*Established and directed a network of over 35 agents and distributors worldwide.
*Developed and implemented a successful sales and marketing strategy which became the foundation for a fully subscribed IPO in 1988.

EDUCATION
M.A. ZOOLOGY The University of South Florida, Tampa, FL
B.S. BIOLOGY Florida Southern College, Lakeland, FL

CONTINUING EDUCATION
DYEING AND FINISHING FUNDAMENTALS
North Carolina State University, Raleigh, NC 1992
LEADING AND MANAGING PEOPLE
Columbia University, NYC 1989
FUNDAMENTALS OF PLASTICS MATERIALS AND PROCESSING Society of Plastics Engineers. 1999

PROFESSIONAL CREDENTIALS
2010 Wollastonite chapter: *Functional Fillers for Plastics*. 2nd Ed. M. Xanthos (Ed).
2006 Wollastonite chapter: *Industrial Minerals & Rocks*. 7$^{th.\ ed.}$
   Wollastonite: Legacy in Reinforcement. Functional Fillers for Plastics 2006. Presentation and Proceedings
   Wollastonite: Strength in Legacy. 2nd Annual International Conference on Fillers for Polymers. Presentation and Proceedings.

2003 Wollastonite: Functional Filler for Coatings. Presentation to Los Angeles Society for Coatings Technology
2002 Wollastonite: A Non-traditional Filler for PVC. Presentation and Proceedings for Vinytech 2002, Chicago, IL.

The Advantages of Wollastonite, a Non-traditional Filler, in Fluorohydrocarbon (FKM) elastomers.
Presentation and Proceedings of the Rubber Div. of American Chemical Society
2002-2003 Functional Silicate Fillers Series (6 articles). Robinson and Ciullo in *Paint & Coatings Industry Magazine*
1985-2006 Numerous presentations globally on the use of inorganic pigments and fillers worldwide.

PUBLICATIONS: Wollastonite and functional filler articles have appeared in *American Paint & Coatings Journal; Polymer, Paint & Colour Journal (United Kingdom); American Ceramic Society; European Coatings Journal; and Ceramic Technology International*

PATENT: Robinson, S. and D.Craig. "Reinforcement of Ceramic Bodies with Wollastonite, Specifically Reinforcement of Sanitaryware Bodies." Patent Number: 6,037,288. Granted March 2000.

PROFESSIONAL ASSOCIATIONS: Prior to career retirement.
Society of Plastics Engineers (SPE), PMAD Div. Board member and former Treasurer
Piedmont Section of Federation of Societies for Coatings Technology (former officer and Past-President)
Society of Automotive Engineers
American Chemical Society
Society of Mining Engineers
American Ceramic Society

CIVIC INTERESTS:
Past Executive Board Member of the Corpus Christi, TX Chamber of Commerce(1989-1990): Head of Education Committee for the CC Board(1990).
Pantops Citizen Advisory Committee Member (2017-2019) Charlottesville, VA
President, Riverside Village Community Association (2019-2022) Charlottesville, VA
Former Board Member, Elkton (VA) Welcome Center Committee (2010-2011)
Former Instructor of Poetry Appreciation & Critique UVA-OLLI (ca 2012-2016)
Visiting Instructor of Poetry at UVA College at Wise (2015, 2017, 2019)
Facilitator of Poetry Understanding at The Collonades (Sunrise Senior Living Facility) Charlottesville, VA [2012-present]
Workshop on Poetry Critique and Composition. Writer House Center. Charlottesville,VA

PAST AWARDS: Former career and civic participations
Peabody Award given by PMAD Div. of SPE (2002)
Who's Who in Plastics and Polymers (2000)
YWCA/YMCA "Ys" Women and Men in Careers Award (1989) Corpus Christi, TX.

INTERESTS:
Creative writing (now a professional pursuit); astronomy; fly tying; birding; reading

www.ingramcontent.com/pod-product-compliance
Lightning Source LLC
Chambersburg PA
CBHW031625210526
45464CB00004B/1757